PRAGUE

Everyman MapGuides

D1579489

Welcome to Prague!

This opening fold-out contains a g ... se
the 6 large districts discussed in th. ... mation,
handy tips and useful addresses.

Discover Prague through 6 districts and 6 maps

A Staré Město

B Josefov / Letná

C Hradčany

D Malá Strana

E Nové Město / Vyšehrad

F Vinohrady / Žižkov

For each district there is a double-page of addresses (restaurants – listed in
ascending order of price – cafés, bars, tearooms, music venues and shops),
followed by a fold-out map for the relevant area with the essential places to
see (indicated on the map by a star ★). These places are by no means all that
Prague has to offer, but to us they are unmissable. The grid-referencing
system (**A** B2) makes it easy for you to pinpoint addresses quickly on the map.

Transportation and hotels in Prague

The last fold-out consists of a transportation map and 4 pages of practical
information that include a selection of hotels.

Thematic index

Lists all the sites and addresses featured in this guide.

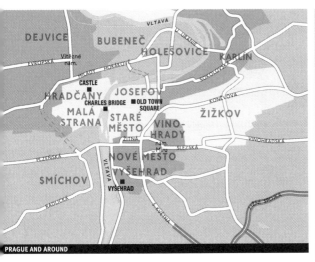

PRAGUE AND AROUND

BAROQUE

After the victory of the Catholics (1620), the baroque movement in Prague acquired a politico religious significance. It gradually freed itself from the constraints of the Counter-Reformation and in the 18th century, starte to adorn Prague's most beautiful palaces.

St Savior's Church
→ *Klementinum* (**A** B2)
So-called Jesuit baroque style (Carlo Lurago 1638-4

St Nicholas' Church in Malá Strana (**D** D1)
The crowning glory of religious baroque (Dientzenhofer, 1703–55)

Baroque palaces
→ *Nerudova* (**D** C1)

SECESSION

The Czech branch of Art Nouveau (late 19th-early 20th century) influenced by the German Jugendsti and the Viennese Sezession. Wrought iron, mosaics, stained glass and adornment with organic forms embellish façades and interiors.

Municipal House (**A** F1)
Interior decoration by Ale Mucha, Mařatka...

Hotel Europa (**E** C1)
→ *Vaclavské náměstí 25*
Decor in the café.

CUBISM

The only city where Cubist architecture became a reality.

Black Virgin House (**A** E1)
Cubist museum in a hou designed by Josef Gočár (1911–12).

Cubist houses (**E** A5)
Josef Chochol (1911–13).

Tramway rental
→ *Patočkova 4*
Tel. 223 343 349
(reservations)
Price: 3000 Kč/hr

By boat
Prague Steamboat Company (PPS) (**A** B2)
→ *Rasinovo nabrezi (Prague 2)* Tel. 224 931 013
Mid March-Oct: daily 3.30pm
Price 250–350 Kč.
Duration: 1 ½ hrs
Trips to Štvanice Island, returning via Vyšehrad, on the Vltava, on board a steamboat. Other routes available.

By balloon
Ballooning CZ
→ *Na vrcholu 7, Prague 3*
Tel. 284 861 198
Price: 3,800–4,200 Kč/ pers
Fly over Prague in an airship. Departs from the Konopiště (½ hr from Smíchov station) or the Karlštejn castles (1 hr away from the main station).

Guided tours
Information from the PIS.

Pragotour (**A** D1)
→ *Staroměstské náměsti 1*
Tel. 224 482 562 or 236 002 562
Guided tours in several languages.

Prague Walks
→ *Nezamyslova 7*
Tel. 261 214 603
Walks with a theme: 'Pubs' 'The Velvet Revolution', 'The Ghosts of Prague', etc.

MUSEUMS, MONUMENTS

Opening hours
Generally open Tue-Sun from 10am to 6pm (or 5pm); late opening night (9pm) on Thursday in some museums.

Prices
Varies from one museum to the other (30–100 Kč).

Reductions
For students and groups.

Prague Card
→ *Price 690 Kč for 3 days*
(*Čedok, travel agencies*)
Unlimited access to public

transport and 44 museums.

Free admission
First Monday of month in the National Museum (**F** A3), first Thursday of month for the Prague City Museum (**B** F4), one day per month for the Modern Art Museum (**B** E1), and for Kinský Palace (**A** D1).

RESTAURANTS

Opening hours
Lunch from 11am to 3pm, dinner from 6pm to 11pm. Reservation advisable in high season.

What to eat
In snack bars or self-service buffet (*samoobsluha* or *Automat*)
Chlebícky (various pies), sandwiches, hamburgers, *knedlíky* (sliced potato balls).
In the street: food stalls
Párky (hot dogs), *klobásy* (grilled sausages), *bramboraky* (potato pancakes).

PASSAGEWAY IN STARÉ MĚSTO

VIEW OF THE BRIDGES

PASSAGEWAYS AND GALLERIES

Staré Město is an astonishing maze, which can be crossed without seeing a street.

Passageways
Bare, narrow, dark and humid, these old passageways are an essential part of the city's structure. Between **Karlova** (**A** C2), **Michalská**, **Jilská** and **Melantrichova** (**A** D2).

Galleries
Luxurious, architecturally daring galleries built at the end of the 19th century.
Koruna Pasáž (**E** C1)
Lucerna Pasáž (**E** C1)

CITY PROFILE

■ Capital of Czech Republic ■ 1.2 million inhabitants ■ 10 districts ■ Temperatures: 29°F/Jan 67°F/July ■ Currency : the crown, *Koruna* (Kč), non convertible ($1 = 26 Kč ; £1 = 46 Kč) at the time of printing

THE DISTRICTS OF PRAGUE

TOURIST INFO

Prague Information Service (PIS)
➔ *Old Town Hall / Na Příkopě 20 / Bridge Tower/ Central Station*
Tel. 12 444
Mon-Fri 9am–7pm (6pm winter); Sat-Sun 9am–5pm (3pm Sat winter)
www.pis.cz
The municipal tourist office (four branches). Info, bookings for shows and hotels (AVE agency).
Čedok (**A** E2)
➔ *Na Příkopě 18*
Tel. 224 197 643
Mon-Fri 9am–6pm
Ticket sales for concerts and shows. Guided tours, excursions.

WWW.

➔ *czechcenter.com*
American website. Info on Czech culture, business, travel tips, etc.

➔ *czechtourism.com*
➔ *visitczechia.cz*
Official website of the Czech Tourist Authority.
➔ *a-zprague.cz*
Extensive info (English)
Good cultural magazine
➔ *www.praguepost.cz*
Embassies
➔ *www.usembassy.cz*
US embassy in Prague.
Tel. 257 530 663
➔ *www.britain.cz*
UK embassy in Prague.
Tel. 257 402 111
Internet cafés
Spika (**F** B1)
➔ *Dlážděná 4*
www.netcafe.spika.cz
Daily 8am–midnight

VIEWS OF THE CITY

Petřín Belvedere (**D** C3)
Reached by the 299 steps of this miniature replica of the Eiffel Tower.
Old Town Hall (**A** D2)
Its 14th-century Gothic tower dominates the Old Town Square.
Old Town Bridge Tower (**A** B2)
Ornate sculptural decoration and glorious view of the Vltava.
Vyšehrad Hill (**E** B6)
Quiet spot for a picnic, with unbeatable views of the city and its hills.
Powder Tower (**A** F1)
➔ *Náměstí Republiky*
View of the Royal Way from the tower.

PARKS AND GARDENS

Opening hours
Open 10am to 6pm. Many gardens and castles are closed Nov 1-March 31. There are pretty gardens on the islands of Slovanský, Kampa, Střelecký and Dětský.
Stromovska Park
➔ *Nádraží Holesovice*
subway then tram 5, 12 or 17
The largest park in Prague (990 acres), formerly the

royal hunting ground. Wood, paths and ponds (skating in winter).
Royal Garden (**C** D2)
Renaissance garden with lawns, fountains, elaborate hedges and sculptures.
Letná Park (**B** B2)
Huge plateau, turned into a park in 1858. Views of the Vltava and the Josefov.

ALTERNATIVE TRANSPORT

By tramway
Lines n° 17, 22 and 23 (regular lines serving Prague's main monuments.)
Tourist tram n° 91 and historic tramway line
➔ *April-end Oct: Sat, Sun and public hols, noon–6pm. Tickets sold on board (25 Kč; 10 Kč for under 10s)*
Trip on an early 20th-century wooden tram: Old Town, New Town and Jewish Quarter. Departs from Exhibition Park.

Welcome to Prague!

A Staré Město

B Josefov / Letná

C Hradčany

D Malá Strana

E Nové Město / Vyšehrad

F Vinohrady / Žižkov

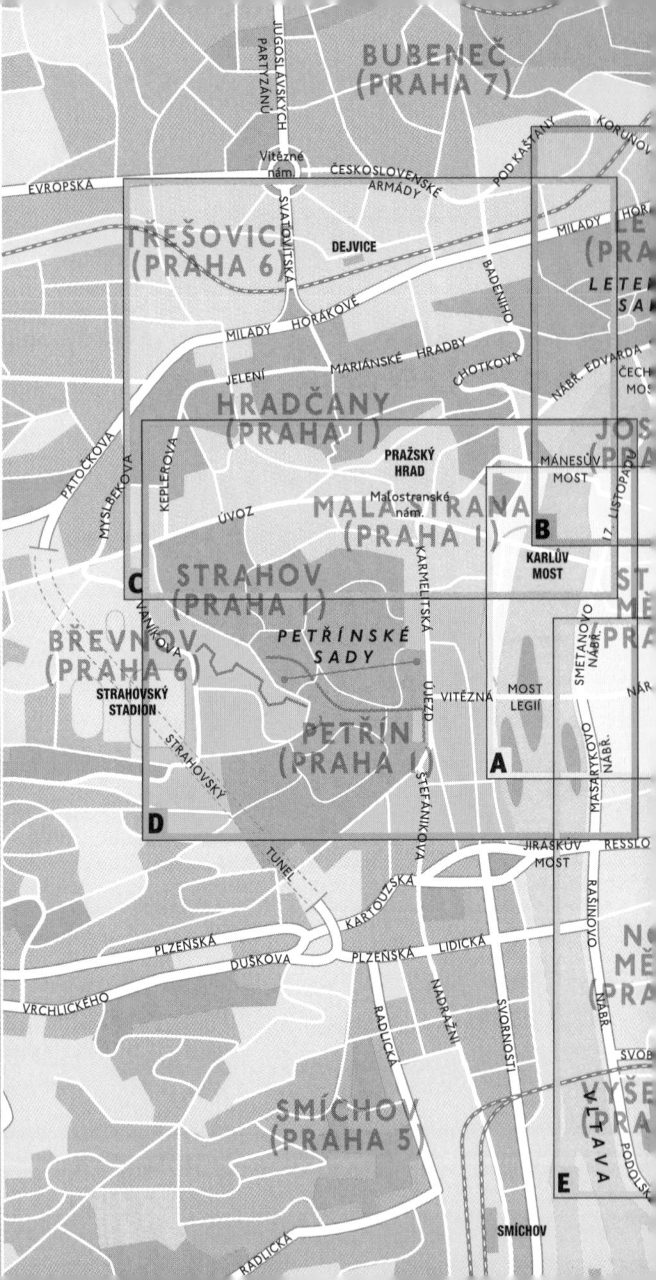

BUBENEČ
(PRAHA 7)

JUGOSLÁVSKÝCH PARTYZÁNŮ

Vítězné nám.

ČESKOSLOVENSKÉ ARMÁDY

EVROPSKÁ

POD KAŠTANY

KORUNO

MILADY

HOŘ

PRA

TŘEŠOVICE
(PRAHA 6)

DEJVICE

SVATOVÍTSKÁ

BADENÍHO

LETEN

SA

MILADY HORÁKOVÉ

MARIÁNSKÉ HRADBY

CHOTKOVA

NÁBŘ. EDVARDA

ČECH

MOS

JELENÍ

HRADČANY
(PRAHA 1)

PRAŽSKÝ HRAD

JOS
PRA

MÁNESŮV MOST

KEPLEROVA

ÚVOZ

Malostranské nám.

MALÁ STRANA
(PRAHA 1)

B

KARLŮV MOST

ST
MĚ
PRA

PATOČKOVA

MYSLBEKOVA

C

STRAHOV
(PRAHA 1)

KARMELITSKÁ

SMETANOVO NÁBŘ.

17. LISTOPADU

BŘEVNOV
(PRAHA 6)

VANÍČKOVA

PETŘÍNSKÉ SADY

UJEZD

VÍTĚZNÁ

MOST LEGIÍ

NÁR

A

STRAHOVSKÝ STADION

STRAHOVSKÝ

PETŘÍN
(PRAHA 1)

ŠTEFÁNIKOVA

MASARYKOVO NÁBŘ.

D

TUNEL

JIRÁSKŮV MOST

RESSLO

KARTOUZSKÁ

PLZEŇSKÁ LIDICKÁ

RAŠÍNOVO

N
MĚ
PRA

PLZEŇSKÁ

DUŠKOVA

NÁDRAŽNÍ

SVORNOSTI

VRCHLICKÉHO

RADLICKÁ

VYŠE
PRA

SMÍCHOV
(PRAHA 5)

VLTAVA

PODOLS

E

RADLICKÁ

SMÍCHOV

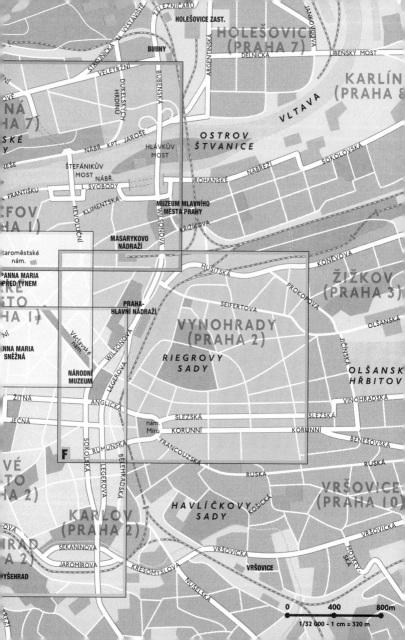

MALOSTRANSKÉ NÁMĚSTÍ

Tel. 224 227 832
→ Na Příkopě 16
Tel. 224 215 031
Prague Tourist Center
→ Rytířská 12, Můstek
subway Tel. 2423 6047

CALENDAR

January
International dance week.
April
→ April 30
End of winter: burning of
brooms (witches' stakes)
and dancing (Kampa
Island).
May
→ May 1
Spring festival: carnival
parades, fair in Střelecký
Ostrov, concerts in parks.
→ May 5
Commemoration of the
Prague Uprising.
→ May 15
International book fair.
June
→ Third weekend
Summer solstice: period

costumes, open-air shows.
July–August
Free concerts (gardens);
displays using water and
light (Exhibition Palace);
theater and puppets
Střelecký Island, May-Sep).
September
→ The whole month
Autumn fair: theater,
music, puppets.
→ September 28
Feast of St Wenceslas:
a national celebration.
November
→ November 17
Anniversary of the Velvet
Revolution: demos around
Wenceslas Square.
December
→ The whole month
Christmas markets (Old
Town Square).
→ December 5–6
Eve of St Nicholas' day:
distribution of candies,
recitals and songs.
→ Week of December 25
Christmas week: market in
tents in the city's streets.

→ December 26
Swimming competition in
the Vltava, with water at
37° F (3°C)!

TELEPHONE

From USA / UK
→ 011/00 + 420 (Czech Rep)
+ 9-digit number starting
with 2 (Prague)
From Prague
→ 00 + country code + city
code + number
Public telephones
Phone cards
→ Card 200 to 300 Kč
(in post offices, tobacco
shops, kiosks)
Post offices
→ 2.40 Kč/unit
Twenty percent cheaper
than the phone boxes.
Useful numbers
Police
→ 156 (city), 158 (country)
Assistance, ambulance
→ 155
Fire brigade
→ 150

MUSIC IN PRAGUE

Classical concerts
Are played throughout
the year, in the city's
innumerable churches.
Details from Čedok and
the PIS.
Chapel of Mirrors
→ Klementinum (A C2)
Handel, Bach, Mozart,
Beethoven, in this
stunning chapel, usually
closed to the public.
**St Nicholas'
Church (A D1)**
→ Staroměstské náměstí
Organ recitals, excellent
acoustics.
Prague Spring
→ May 12-June 2
Tel. 257 312 547
(bookings)
Price 250–2,500 Kč
One of the most
prestigious classical
music festivals in the
world. Concerts in
theaters, churches and
monuments. Always
starts on May 12
(anniversary of the
death of the Czech
composer Šmetana).
Verdi Festival
→ Aug-Sept
Three weeks of opera
dedicated to Verdi.
Autumn Festival
→ Two weeks in Sep
Tel. 222 540 484
(reservations)
Classical concerts in the
Rudolfinum (B A4).
Mozart in Prague
→ All year
www.mozart.cz
Tribute from the city that
best understood him.
**International Jazz
Festival**
→ www.agharta.cz
Local and international
stars in concert in the
Lucerna Palace (E C1).

…man cellars

…avoid flooding by the …ava, Staré Město was …sed in the 18th century. …e vaulted cellars were …ce the ground floors of …man villas.

…use of the Three White …ses (A D2)
…Malé náměstí 3

…graffito

…chnique imported from …ly to imitate stone …sing black mortar with …rough white coating. …6th century).

…use …f the Minute' (A D1)
…Staroměstské náměstí 2
…blical scenes in sgraffito …arly 17th century).

CAFÉ LOUVRE

POTREFENÁ HUSA

BEER

Hospoda, pivnice

Budvar, Staropramen, Kelt, Pilsner, Pilsen Urquell on draft (around 30 Kč / pint), served in a pivnice or hospada (Czech pub or beer hall) generally shrouded in smoke.

Custom

Big tables are shared. Do not hesitate to ask permission to sit at a table that is already occupied. To order place a glass beer in front of you.Beware, once a glass is empty, a waiter immediately replaces it with a full one unless you ask him not to.

…afés (kavárna)
…ndwiches, cakes.
Czech pubs or beer halls …ospoda, pivnice)
…brasseries, wine bars …árna)
…ernational dishes and …ech specialties.

…l, tips
…e aperitifs and nibbles …ved automatically are not …ually free (don't hesitate …refuse them). Some …staurants add a cover …arge for bread (check if this …written in the menu).
…: 10% of the total price.

HOPPING

…pening hours

…nks, bureaux de change …nks: Mon-Fri 8am-5pm …r 6pm). Foreign exchange …ices: daily 9am-11pm.
…ores
…enerally open Mon-Fri 9am-…m; Sat 9am-1pm. Many …ores close at lunchtime.

Department stores
Mon-Sat 9am-8pm;
Sun 10am-6pm.

Payment
Credit cards
Now accepted in most stores in the tourist area.
Customs
All purchases over 500 Kč are subject to a tax. Keep all receipts.
Sales
After Christmas.

Department stores
Koruna Palác (E C1)
Major western brands.
Kotva (B D4)
The biggest and most popular (five floors).
Tesco (E B1)
→ Národní Třída 26
Selection of Czech products.
Bílá Labuť' (A E3)
→ Na Poříčí / Václavské nám.
The oldest (1939). Furniture and interior decoration.

Markets
Prague market
→ Holešovice
Mon-Fri 9am-4pm

Held in a former slaughterhouse. Everything is on sale, from fruit and vegetables to spare car parts.
St Havel's market (A D2)
In the heart of the city: fresh produce, crafts...
Flea market (B F1)
→ Holešovice Tržnice
Vltavska subway
Sat 9am-5pm
The Czechs clear out their attics and bring the contents here!

SHOWS

Information on shows
Přehled
Listing of concerts, shows, plays (published every month by the PIS).
Prague Post
→ In kiosks on Wed
Cultural news, 'What's on' (in English)
The Prague Pill
→ Free weekly of the tourist office, in English
Cultural update, tourist info...

Black theater
All the magic of Prague reflected in its shadow plays, mime and puppets.
Ta Fantastika (A C2)
→ Karlova 8 Tel. 2222 1366
Tales of fantasy.
Jiří Srnec (A D3)
→ Národní 20 Tel. 257 921 83?
Show at 8.30pm
Prague's most prestigious black theater troupe.
National Puppet Theater (A C1)
→ Žatecká 1 Tel. 2481 9322
Thu-Tue 8pm
Puppet shows for young and old like.

Reservations
At the PIS or the Čedok (see Tourist Info). But also:
Ticketpro
→ Václavské nám. 38
Tel. 296 329 999
www.ticketpro.cz (English)
Many outlets in the center.
BTI (Bohemia Ticket International)
www.ticketsbti.cz
→ Malé náměstí 13

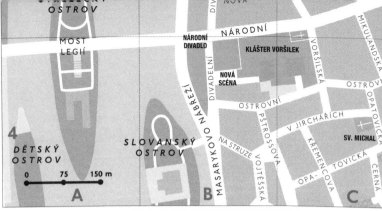

KINSKÝ PALACE

CHURCH OF OUR LADY OF TÝN

Charles Bridge (A A2)
The oldest bridge in the city (1357), and the only link between the two banks until the 19th century. Thirty statues of saints (1683–1714) line both sides, as a splendid baroque guard of honor for the royal entourage as it passed on its way to the Castle. In the center is the statue of St John Nepomuk (1683), on the spot where Wenceslas IV's guards hurled him into the Vltava for refusing to divulge the Queen's confession. Ghostly at night, when the light of the street lamps projects the martyred saints' shadows onto the paving stones.

★ **Klementinum (A** C2)
→ Křížovnické / Marianské náměstí Tel. 221 663 248 Mon-Fri 2–7pm; Sat-Sun and public hols 10am–7pm. Guided tours by appointment
The largest architectural complex after the Castle. In their zeal to convert the Czech people to Catholicism, the Jesuits took possession of 32 houses, 3 churches, 2 gardens and a convent to build their university, but the latter's baroque and rococo splendors are now only enjoyed by authorized members of the National Library. Do not miss St Savior's Church and its baroque porch (Caratti 1648–9), inspired by the

Gesù in Rome, or the Italian Chapel (1590–1600) with its astonishing oval ground-plan heralding the baroque style (entrance on Karlova St). The Hall and Chapel of Mirrors are opened for concerts and exhibitions.

★ **Old Town Hall (A** D2)
→ Staroměstské náměstí 1 Tel. 224 482 629 (224 810 758 for Town Hall Gallery) Mon 11am–6pm; Tue-Sun 9am–6pm (5pm Nov-March)
The assassination of Wenceslas (929), the coronation of Charles IV (1346), the execution of the Hussite chiefs (1621): Old Town Square has witnessed some of the most decisive moments in

Prague's history. Got baroque, Renaissanc Art Nouveau styles pleasantly interming Tourists mill around t Hall's astronomical c entranced by the sta of the 12 apostles pa on the hour above th two dials.

★ **St Nicolas' Church (A** D1)
→ Staroměstské / Paří Daily 10am–5pm (4pm March); clocktower: Ap 10am–6pm
One of the earliest ex of Prague's baroque reflecting the final re from the Counter-Reformation yoke. Th flow upward with gre

A

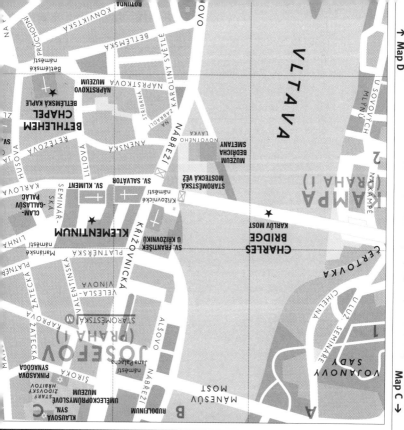

KLEMENTINUM

CHARLES BRIDGE

Winding alleys, galleries and passage-ways. The best way to escape the ceaseless throng of tourists is by getting lost in this maze of tiny streets. From Charles Bridge to Old Town Square, Staré Město, the historic heart of the city, is bursting with a panoply of styles: Roman cellars, dark Gothic towers, Renaissance houses and exuberant baroque façades. The weight of history is ever-present. In Old Town Square the proud statue of Jan Hus revives the memory of the execution of ten Hussite leaders, who were captured by the Catholics in the Battle of the White Mountain (1620).

U DVOU KOČEK | KONVIKT

RESTAURANTS

Klub architektů (**A** C3)
→ *Betlémské náměstí 169/5a* Tel. 224 401 214
Daily 11.30am–11pm
Go down the steps in the courtyard opposite the Bethlehem Chapel, deep into the bowels of the earth, before reaching a series of vaulted cellars. The decor flirts with modernity, but the thick stone 12th-century walls make it impossible to forget that Jan Hus once preached here. Czech specialties like *betlémská směs* (pork and vegetable stew), salads and international cuisine. Some tables in the courtyard in summer. À la carte 220 Kč.

Kamenný Most (**A** B2)
→ *Smetanovo nábřeží 195 (entrance on Karlovy Lazné gallery)* Tel. 224 097 100
Daily 11.30am–midnight
Taxi-boat: 602 224 223
Czech and international cuisine try to outshine each other with flair and imagination in Emperor Charles' old cellar, situated at the foot of the bridge. Outside, a terrace with a view of the Vltava. No access by car, but there's a taxi-boat service to avoid the traffic jams of the town

center. À la carte 600 Kč.

Mlýnec (**A** B2)
→ *Novotného lávka 9*
Tel. 221 082 208
Daily noon–3pm, 5.30–11pm
Prague is the latest conquest for 'ethno-chic' and Mlýnec offers a tour of the world's cuisines (Canadian lobster, French foie gras with chutney, salmon kebab in chili sauce, Italian panacotta). Very elegant setting with a view of Charles Bridge. À la carte 1,000 Kč.

U modré růže (**A** D2)
→ *Rytířská 16*
Tel. 224 225 873
Mon-Sat 11.30am–11.30pm; Sun 6–11.30pm
A massive 15th-century Gothic cellar for a truly romantic evening. Elaborate and exquisite cuisine (mixed grilled fish, ostrich fillet with kiwis, alligator steak). Piano music in the background. Around 1,000 Kč.

CZECH PUBS

U Dvou Koček (**A** D3)
→ *Uhelný trh 10*
Tel. 224 221 692
Daily 11am–11pm
For centuries Pilsner Urquell has flowed like water in the 'Two Cats'. The white walls display old posters advertising the

RNA OBECNÍ DŮM | THEATER OF THE ESTATES | ST HAVEL'S MARKET

brand and some vintage photos. On the tables are piles of glass mats: take one, put it down and a beer appears, then another, and so on until saturation point. In the background, accordion tunes and the animated conversations of the locals. Good Czech cooking: *polévka* (soup) with cabbage, *knedlíky* (dumplings), *guláš* (beef in sauce). À la carte 195 Kč.

Pivnice Radegast (A E1)
→ *Templová 2*
Tel. 222 328 237
Daily 11am–midnight
The cloud of smoke, loud voices and laughter of the high-spirited customers set the tone more than the nondescript decor. Radegast (Moravian beer) on draft to wash down the large helpings of food (one of the best *guláš* in town). A pub rapidly growing in popularity. 150–185 Kč/dish.

CAFÉS, PATISSERIE

Konvikt (A C3)
→ *Bartolomějská 11*
Tel. 224 232 427
Mon-Fri 9am–1am;
Sat-Sun noon–1am
No trendy decor here, just some dark wooden tables and chairs for the

lively locals, who laugh, smoke, drink and nibble on plates of breaded cheese (a Czech specialty) or marinated herrings. For more peace and quiet, head for the room by the courtyard or the one in the cellar.

**Kavárna
Obecní dům (A** F1)
→ *Náměstí Republiky 5*
Tel. 222 002 763
Daily 7.30am–11pm
One of the city's most spectacular cafés. Located in the former Town Hall, it has been superbly restored to its 19th-century glory: period candelabras, big mirrors, swathes of marble and metal, waiters in costume. Elegant ladies, passing tourists and businessmen mingle for a breather over a coffee (*káva* or *kafe*) or a pastry. Internet corner also available.

Odkolek (A D2)
→ *Rytířská 12 (no tel.)*
Mon-Fri 7am–10pm; Sat 8am–10pm (10am Sun)
This shop belongs to a chain of patisseries/ bakeries that sells very good, inexpensive breads and the freshest *sacher torte* (chocolate cake), *jablkový závin* (strudel) and *koláče* (fruit and poppy-seed tarts).

NIGHTCLUBS, THEATER

Double trouble (A D2)
→ *Melantrichova 17*
Tel. 221 632 414
Daily 7pm–4am
A nightclub very popular with expatriates. In a maze of vaulted rooms are two bars, video screens and rock-pop music played at full volume.

Karlovy lázné (A B2)
→ *Novotného lávka 5*
Tel. 222 220 502
Daily 9pm–5am
The former public baths transformed into a gigantic nightclub arranged over four levels, with three bars, three dance floors (house, hardcore, hip-hop and 1960s rock), as well as three bars and a lounge on the fourth level.

**Theater of
the Estates (A** E2)
(Stavoské divadlo)
→ *Ovocný trh 1*
Tel. 224 214 339 / 215 001 (reservations)
Prague's oldest theater, built by Count Nostic in 1781. It was here, in 1787, that Mozart's *Don Giovanni* was first performed. Two centuries later Miloš Forman filmed *Amadeus* on the same spot. The theater was completely restored in

1992. Today it houses ballets, classical concerts and opera in rotation.

SHOPPING

**St Havel's
Market (A** D2)
→ *Havelská*
Mon-Fri 8am–6pm
Havelské Město has been the domain of traders since the 13th century, and its market is still one of the prettiest in Prague. Colorful fruit, flower and vegetable stalls. Also Czech and Moravian crafts on sale: dolls in traditional dress, wooden toys, embroidered fabrics and table linen.

Modernista (A C3)
→ *Konviktská 5*
Tel. 220 220 113
www.modernista.cz Mon-Fri 2pm–6pm; Sat 11am–4pm or by appointment
Gallery exhibiting furniture and accessories from the first half of the 20th century. Art Deco, Czech Cubism, Bauhaus... A retro fashion to rediscover.

Anagram (A E1)
→ *Tyn 4*
Tel. 224 895 737 Mon-Sat 10am–8pm (6pm Sun)
Excellent English-language bookstore with an extensive list of Anglo-Saxon and translated Central European titles.

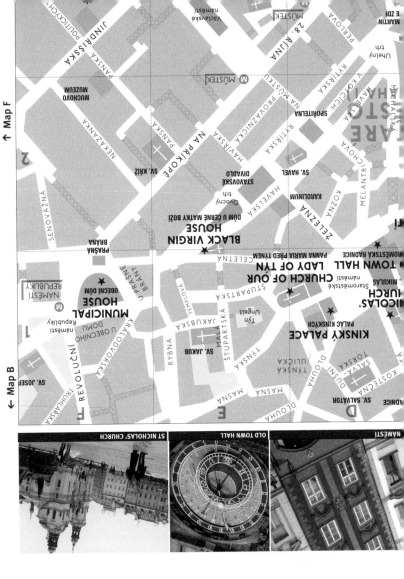

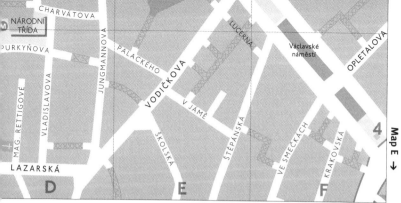

VIRGIN HOUSE

MUNICIPAL HOUSE

BETHLEHEM CHAPEL

, partly due to the lack
ace available to the
ects K. I. and Ch.
zenhofer. Finished in
in a narrow street, the
h was shorn of the
unding buildings, and
hiteness of its
mental façade now
inates the square.
nous interior, with
essive stuccos by
ard Spinetti; frescos by
a Damiam Asam.

alé náměstí (A D2)
triangular 'Little
re', mixing Gothic
es with Renaissance
ito façades. In the
r is a well, adorned
a superb Renaissance
ght-iron grill (1560).

★ Kinský Palace (A D1)
→ Staroměstské náměstí 12
Tel. 224 810 758
Tue-Sun 10am–6pm
Magnificent collection of
graphic art (from the Middle
Ages to the present day)
from the National Gallery,
a fine rococo palace.

★ Church of
Our Lady of Týn (A D1)
→ Staroměstské náměstí 14
Currently being restored
The city's most important
Gothic sanctuary (1365–
1470). Its two 260-ft high
towers dominate the
square, seemingly piercing
the sky with their pointed
spires. The decoration
in this symbol of the
Reformation was given the

baroque treatment in the
17th century. Do not miss
the tympanum of the north
portal and its Crucifixion.

★ Municipal House (A F1)
→ Náměstí Republiky 5
Tel. 222 002 100
Guided tours: check for times
www.obecnidum.cz
Czech Art Nouveau in all
its splendor. Aleš, Mucha,
Maŕatka... the era's greatest
talents were mobilized
between 1902 and 1911 to
decorate its sumptuous
salons, concert halls, café
and restaurant.

★ Black
Virgin House (A E1)
→ Celetná 34
Tel. 222 321 459
Tue-Sun 10am–6pm

On the fourth and fifth floors
is the Museum of Czech
Cubism, set in a Cubist
house (1911–12) by Josef
Gocar. Painting, sculpture,
furniture. The other floors,
used for exhibitions, are
currently closed due to the
transfer of the National
Gallery to the outskirts of
Prague.

★ Bethlehem
Chapel (A C2)
→ Betlemské náměstí
Tue-Sun 10am–5.30pm
(10.30–6pm in summer)
Faithful reconstruction
(1950) of Jan Hus' chapel
(14th century). The
building's simplicity is
indicative of the preacher's
reforming ideas.

ST AGNES' CONVENT

ST JACOB'S CHURCH

★ **Rudolfinum** (**B** A4)
→ *Alšovo nábřeží 12*
Tel. 227 059 111 / 352 (res.)
In 1874 Prague finally boasted a concert hall fit for its musical reputation. Dvořák conducted the premiere of his 'New World Symphony' here in 1896. Thanks to its exceptional acoustics, it has become the seat of the Czech Philharmonic Orchestra and the venue for the Spring Festival.

★ **Museum of Decorative Arts** (**B** B4)
→ *Listopadu 2*
Tel. 251 093 111
Tue-Sun 10am–6pm
Central Europe's most important collection of decorative arts, from the Czech Republic and beyond. Fabrics, Bohemian glass, pottery, jewelry, from the Middle Ages to the late 19th century.

★ **Old Jewish Cemetery** (**B** B4)
→ *Široká 3 (same ticket as National Jewish Museum)*
Eroded by age, the tombstones are coming loose or being swallowed up by the earth. Europe's oldest Jewish resting place houses the bodies of the Ghetto Jews, imprisoned there until their death. One of the first sepulchers was for Rabbi Avigdor Karo (April 23,

1493). The burials were stopped by order of Joseph II in 1787, out of fear of contagion from the plague. Thousands of tourists now throng the cemetery, sometimes forgetting that this is still a sacred place for the Jewish community.

★ **National Jewish Museum** (**B** B4)
→ *Maiselova 10 (Maisel syn.); Široká 3 (Pinkas syn.); Vězeňská 1 (Spanish syn.); U Starého hřbitova (Klaus syn.) Tel. 222 317 191*
April-Oct: Sun-Fri 9am–6pm; Nov-March: Sun-Fri 9am–4.30pm. Closed Jewish hols
More than 40,000 works of art and 100,000 documents,

are to be found in the buildings that survived destruction of the ghe in the late 19th centur 1,000 years of history from one of Europe's most important Jewish communities. You will exhibition devoted to festivals and tradition the Klaus synagogue, 6,000 religious object the Maisel synagogue a profoundly moving memorial to the victim Nazism in the Pinkas synagogue. Names of 77,297 Jews from Mora and Bohemia who die concentration camps engraved on the walls

B

VLTAVA

NÁBŘEŽÍ EDVARDA BENEŠE

ČECHŮV

HANAVSKÝ PAVILON

LETNÁ PARK
LETENSKÉ SADY

LETENSKÝ TUNEL

MUZEJNÍ

NÁRODNÍ MU

LET

LETNÁ (PRAHA 7)

OVENECKÁ

DOBROV

JIREČKOVA

MILADY HORÁKOVÉ

STADIÓN
SPARTA
PRAHA

MILADY

Letenské náměstí

VELETR

SOCHAŘSKÁ

OVENECKÁ

ŠMERALOVA

HAVANSKÁ

ČECHOVA

SLADKOVA

ZÁLICE

JANA

NA VÝŠINÁCH

U SPARTY

KORUNOVAČNÍ

NAD KRÁLOVSKOU
OBOROU

V ROLLANDA

ROMANA TIŠINĚ

NA ZÁTORCE

2

1

RUDOLFINUM

DVOŘÁKOVA SÍŇ

MUSEUM OF DECORATIVE ARTS

NATIONAL JEWISH MUSEU

The only relics of the eventful history of what was one of Europe's most important Jewish communities: six synagogues, cemetery and the Jewish Town Hall, now retrieved by the tourist industry. Nothing remains of the labyrinthine old ghetto: in the 19th century the maze of courtyards and teeming alleyways gave way to wide and graceful avenues. The Renaissance, baroque and Art Nouveau styles rub shoulders on the façades of the upmarket stores in Pařížská. On the opposite bank is Letná Park, a perfect setting for a stroll and, further north, Holešovice, a lively area with its roots in the industrial era.

HANAVSKÝ PAVILÓN

BAROCK

RESTAURANTS

Red, Hot & Blues (B C4)
→ Jakubská 12
Tel. 222 323 364
Daily 9am–11pm
Cajun and Tex-Mex cooking (nachos, fajitas, gumbo, Bourbon pork) and cocktails (piña colada, margarita...). Live blues or jazz bands every night. Breakfast served until 11.30am. Eat in the courtyard in summer. À la carte 480 Kč.

Chez Marcel (B C3)
→ Haštalská 12
Tel. 222 315 676
Mon–Fri 8am–1pm;
Sat–Sun 9am–1am
A small corner of France in the heart of Prague. French and francophiles meet for a drink or meal. Salad niçoise, rabbit in mustard sauce, quiche lorraine, steak with black pepper, tarte tatin. Wine bar in the basement. À la carte 500 Kč.

Hanavský pavilón (B A3)
→ Letenské sady 173
Tel. 233 323 641
Daily 11am–11pm
A lovely rococo hunting pavilion (1891), shrouded in the wood, on top of Letná Hill. On fine days you can sit outside on the very pleasant terrace, with a view of the city and the

Vltava. Game, smoked fish, caviar. À la carte 1,000 Kč.

Pravda (B B4)
→ Pařížská 17
Tel. 222 326 203
Daily noon–1am
A highly sophisticated restaurant near the Old-New Synagogue, with a smart clientele in search of exoticism – the menu includes Italian, Spanish, Vietnamese, Lebanese and Scandinavian dishes. À la carte 1,200–1,500 Kč.

Rybí trh (B C4)
→ Týn Ungelt 5
Tel. 224 895 447
Daily 11am–midnight
Another chic restaurant in a medieval courtyard behind Our Lady of Týn. True, it is pricey but also famous for the quality of its very fresh fish and seafood displayed in the aquarium or on a bed of ice. You choose the way you want it cooked: poached, grilled, fried... Terrace on the courtyard in summer. Dishes 1,100–1,200 Kč.

WINE BAR, CZECH PUB

Švejk (B B4)
→ Široká 20
Tel. 224 813 964
Daily 11am–11pm
This pleasant tavern is one of many places in the

UIS DE SADE

ROXY

BOTANICUS

city paying tribute to the 'good soldier Švejk', hero of the popular novel by Jaroslav Hasek. Wood trim, old posters and vintage prints and good Czech cuisine: *buřtys cibulí* (salami and onion), *bramboračka* (potato soup), *pečené koleno* (shin of pork).
À la carte 300–400 Kč.

U Golema (B B4)
→ *Maiselova 8*
Tel. 222 328 165
Daily 11am–11.30pm
A quiet, restful wine bar, popular with Prague's Jewish community. The strange names of some of the dishes – the 'Rage of the Golem', the 'Rabbi's bag' – refer to the old ghetto legend of the mythical Golem figure. Fish and poultry, as well as vegetarian dishes.
À la carte 400–500 Kč.

CAFÉS

Barock (B B4)
→ *Pařížská 24*
Tel. 222 329 221
Mon-Fri 8.30am–1am (brunch: 8.30–11.30am); Sat-Sun 10am–1pm (brunch: 10am–4pm)
Photos of models on the walls, designer furniture and a hip crowd of both locals and tourists.

Good selection of cigars. Brunch with homemade croissants.

Dolce vita (B B4)
→ *Široká 15*
Tel. 222 329 192
Daily 8am–11.30pm
One of Prague's few Italian cafés, for a real espresso or a creamy cappuccino. Short food menu: panini, ham and melon, mozzarella salad, tiramisù...

BARS, NIGHTCLUBS

Kozička (B C3)
→ *Kozí 1*
Tel. 224 818 308
Mon-Fri noon–4am; Sat-Sun 6pm–4am
Relaxed in the afternoon, lively and youthful at night – thanks, perhaps, to flowing Krušovice (beer on draft from centra Bohemia), and Slivovice (plum brandy). Short food menu (chicken, chili, salads, pork in curry sauce). Carte 360 Kč.

Marquis de Sade (B C4)
→ *Templová 8*
Tel. 222 817 505
Daily 2pm–2am
A huge red room with round tables, patronized by young locals and expatriates eager for a good night out. Lively ambience, lots of tobacco

smoking, strong liquor, Czech beer on draft (Kelt, Krušovice, Velvet) and, sometimes, live music.

Banana Café / La Provence (B C4)
→ *Štupartská 9*
Tel. 222 324 801
Daily 11am–2am
One of the city's most fashionable spots: a café-bar-restaurant, popular with Prague's Anglo-Saxon community and Czech yuppies. Piano bar, drag shows, go-go dancers, heady techno beats, jazz (on Tuesdays). Tapas and breakfast bars. The basement restaurant, La Provence (French cooking) is excellent.
À la carte 800–900 Kč.

Roxy (B C4)
→ *Dlouhá 33*
Tel. 224 826 296
www.roxy.cz
Mon-Sat 10pm–3am
One of the last of Prague's mythical big nightclubs. With cement walls, Roxy looks like an underground parking lot in which techno, drum 'n' bass, house, jungle or trance is played by the best DJs in Europe. Strong liquor copiously consumed to remove any unwelcome inhibitions. Also film screenings, concerts, theater plays.

SHOPPING

Botanicus (B C4)
→ *Týn Ungelt 3*
Tel. 224 895 445
Daily 10am–10pm
The realm of plants and all things natural. Soaps, creams, perfumes, pots-pourris and a selection of craft goods from the Ostrá domain (Lysá nad Labem, to the northwest of Prague), where a 15th-century farm-monastery has been recreated.

Kotva (B D4)
→ *Náměstí Republiky 8*
Tel. 224 801 111
Mon-Fri 9am–8pm; Sat-Sun 10am–7pm (5pm Sun)
There is still a touch of Eastern Europe in the displays of this 1970s department store. You will find just about everything over five floors, especially fine glassware. There is also a foodstore belonging to the Austrian chain Julius Meinl in the basement.

Josef Sudek Galerie (B B4)
→ *Maiselova 2*
Tel. 224 819 098
Daily 11am–6pm
Photographic exhibitions shown all year round. Each one centers around a specific theme or Czech artist.

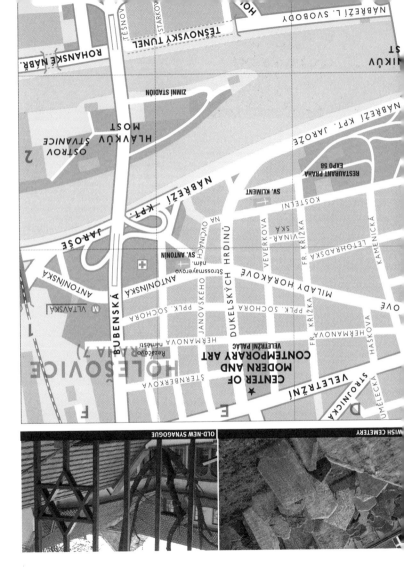

Map labels include: SOUKENICKÁ, TRUHLÁŘSKÁ, ZLATNICKÁ, BISKUPSKÁ, Petrské náměstí, SV. PETR NA POŘÍČÍ, NOVA, FLORENC, MUSEUM OF THE CITY OF PRAGUE — MUZEUM HLAVNÍHO MĚSTA PRAHY, KŘIŽÍKOVA, WILSONOVA, NA POŘÍČÍ, HAVLÍČKOVA, REVOLUČNÍ, SV. JOSEF, NA POŘÍČÍ, NA FLORENCI, AUTOBUSOVÉ NÁDRAŽÍ PRAHA-FLORENC, náměstí Republiky, V CELNICI, OBECNÍ DŮM, NÁMĚSTÍ REPUBLIKY, PRAHA--MASARYKOVO NÁDRAŽÍ, HYBERNSKÁ, HYBERNSKÁ, 0 95 190 m

E CITY MUSEUM

LETNÁ PARK

CENTER OF MODERN AND CONTEMPORARY ART

-New gogue (B B4)
vená 3
opening times as the
al Jewish Museum
f the oldest places of
ip for the European
community (13th
ry). Its dark, unsettling
architecture seems
ect its tumultuous
. The Jews of the
were the victims of
ess massacres and
cutions. It is said that
mains of the Golem,
ing created by the
ogue's rabbi, Löw, lie
building's attic. The
ed tympanum,
ing the foliage of

a fig tree, is a marvel of Gothic art.

★ St Agnes' Convent (B C3)
→ U Milosrdných, 17
Tel. 224 810 628
Tue–Sun 10am–6pm
The National Gallery's medieval art collection from Bohemia and central Europe is shown here, in one of Prague's earliest Gothic buildings (13th century), commissioned by Anežka, sister of Wenceslas I.

★ St Jacob's Church (B C4)
→ Malá Štupartská 6
Mon–Sat 10am–noon,
2–4.45pm
Destroyed by a fire in 1689, the church (14th century) was restored in a baroque

style, although it still retains its soaring Gothic structure. Ottavio Mosto contributed extraordinary stucco compositions to the façade. The tomb of Count Mitrowicz (1714), adorned with sculptures by Brokof, reflects the apogee of Bohemian baroque sculpture. Baroque organ concerts are held here.

★ Museum of the City of Prague (B F4)
→ Na poříčí, 52
Tel. 224 816 772
Tue–Sun 9am–6pm
Contains nearly 500,000 documents on the city's past (from prehistory to the present). Fascinating model of 18th-century Prague.

★ Letná Park (B A1)
Wonderful views of the Old Town and the Vltava from this huge plateau, turned into a park in 1858. To the west, a footbridge links the park to the royal gardens.

★ Center of Modern and Contemporary Art (B E1)
→ Dukelských hrdinů 47
Tel. 224 301 111
Tue–Sun 10am–6pm
Monumental glass and concrete palace (1928) containing works from the 19th and 20th centuries (Picasso, Cézanne, Klimt, Schiele) and retrospectives of the greatest Czech artists (like the painter Bohumil Kubišta).

ST VITUS' CATHEDRAL

OLD ROYAL PALACE

★ Strahov Monastery (C A4)

→ Strahovské nádvoří 1/132
Tel. 220 516 671
Library: daily 9am–noon, 1–5pm.
Museum: Tue-Sun 9am–5pm

Ever since its foundation in 1143, Strahov has collected rare books, manuscripts (of Gregorian chants) and incunabula (9th-century Strahov Gospel). Despite fires and pillages, the collection has remained intact. In the 17th century it was held in the Theology Room (exquisite bookcases in carved walnut, exuberant stuccos). In the Philosophy Room (18th century) are 50-foot-high shelves and a rich fresco by Anton Maulbertsch (1794). The rooms can be observed from the doorway.

★ Loreto Square (C A4)

→ Loretánské náměstí 7
Tel. 220 516 740
Church: Tue-Sun 9am–12.15pm, 1–4.30pm

One of the most beautiful squares in Prague (1703). The monumental Černin Palace (1679) is offset by the elegant rococo façade of Our Lady of Loreto (K. I. Dientzenhofer, 1721). Do not miss the replica of the Italian Santa Casa (1626), dedicated to the cult of the Virgin that marked the reaffirmation of the victory of the Counter-Reformation. The Treasury houses the 'Sun of Prague', a gaudy monstrance set with 6,000 diamonds (1696, by J. B. Fisher von Erlach).

★ Hradčanské Square (C C3)

Extravagant Renaissance and baroque houses overlook the Castle's first courtyard: the Thun-Hohenstein Palace, baroque of Romanesque inspiration; the Bishop's Palace with its rococo façade; the Martinic Palace and its three Gothic houses, converted into Renaissance palaces; the Lobkowicz-Schwarzenberg Palace (1545–63), a masterpiece of the Czech Renaissance.

★ National Gallery Sternberg Palace (C

→ Hradčanské náměstí
Tel. 233 090 570
Tue-Sun 10am–6pm

Contains the Feast of Rose Garlands (Dürer), the Portrait of Eleonor Toledo (Il Bronzino), an many other masterpie by Europe's greatest painters from the 14th 20th centuries.

★ Castle Picture Gallery (C C3)

→ Second courtyard
Tel. 224 373 368
Tue-Sun 10am–6pm

C

STRAHOV MONASTERY

LORETO SQUARE

HRADČANY (PRAHA 1)

ST VÍ... CATH... CASTLE PICTURE... NATIONAL GALLERY / KATEDRÁ...

JÍZDÁRNA

U PRAŠNÉHO MOSTU

JELENÍ

JELENÍ

U BRUSNICE

PATOČKOVA

CUKROVARNICKÁ

MILADY HORÁKOVÉ

NA OŘECHOVCE

MILADY...

POD HRADBAMI

STŘEŠOVICE (PRAHA 6)

DĚLOSTŘELECKÁ

ŽEL. ST. PRAHA DEJVICE

BUŠTĚHRADSKÁ

PEVNOSTNÍ

VÁCLAVKOVA

SVATOVÍTSKÁ

ÚSTAV LETECKÉHO ZDRAVOTNICTVÍ

WUCHTERLOVA

Bachmačské náměstí

KARKOVA

GENERÁLA PÍKY

GENERÁLA PÍKY

DEJVICKÁ

NA HUTÍCH

NA RODNÍ

V P. ČKALOVA

KARKOVA

Vítězné náměstí

DEJVICKÁ

GYMNASIJNÍ

Hradčany

Perched on the side of a hill, the imposing Castle is actually a series of vast structures. Ever since its construction in the 9th century, the citadel has asserted itself as the seat of Bohemian power. It contains a Romanesque royal palace, a Gothic cathedral, Renaissance gardens, baroque churches, a convent... centuries of history and architecture. Outside the citadel, the Royal Way (Nerudova) hurtles down the slopes to the Vltava, leaving a string of vast baroque palaces in its wake. To the west of the citadel, the rococo splendors of Our Lady of Loreto border on Nový Svět, a timeless haven of rustic charm.

LVÍ DVŮR | U ZLATÉ HRUŠKY

RESTAURANTS

Sate (C A4)
→ *Pohořelec 152/3*
Tel. 220 514 552
Daily 11am–10pm
Customers sit at little square tables, in a big, vaulted white room decorated with colorful fabrics. The cooking here is authentic Indonesian, with an excellent *nasi goreng* and chicken with coconut. Around 110 Kč.

Renthauz (C B4)
→ *Loretánská 13/179*
Tel. 220 511 532
Daily 11am–10pm (8.30pm summer)
Have lunch or dinner opposite the gardens of Petřín Hill. On the menu, the classics of Czech cuisine: *vepřo, knedlíky, zelo* (pork, dumplings and cabbage).
À la carte 155–185 Kč.

U zlaté hrušky (C A3)
→ *Nový svět 3/77*
Tel. 220 514 778
Daily 11.30am–3pm, 6.30pm–midnight
The 'Golden Pear' offers elaborate game specialties (duck breast with black pepper, haunch of venison with pears) in the cozy setting of a pretty 16th-century Gothic house standing in one of Prague's most elegant streets. In summer, meals are served under the centuries-old chestnut trees in the garden. Nineteen menus in total, of which four are vegetarian. 190–1,500 Kč.

Lví dvůr (C C3)
→ *U prašného mostu 6/51*
Tel. 224 372 361
Daily 10am–11pm
Soft lighting, exposed beams, sturdy wooden tables, bouquets of flowers: simplicity combined with elegance. On the menu, *pražské selátko*: 'Prague pig' spit-roasted following a Renaissance recipe. Fine Bohemian and Moravian wines that include Pražské Selátko, a champagne wine specially produced for the restaurant. Menu 860 Kč.

Peklo (C A4)
→ *Strahovské nádvoří 132/1*
Tel. 220 516 652
Mon 6pm–midnight; Tue–Sun noon–midnight
'Hell' – this was the monks' nickname for the cellar of the Strahov Monastery. Vaulted rooms, a host of alcoves, and good Czech and international cuisine.
À la carte 900 Kč.

U Cisaŕu (C A4)
→ *Loretánská 5/175*
Tel. 220 518 484 Daily 11am–midnight (1am wine bar)
Near the Castle, 'The

C STARÁ RADNICE

MALÝ BUDDHA

STORE ON THE GOLDEN LANE

Emperors' is housed in a 13th-century building of great character, whose windows look down on the Mala Strana gardens. The wine list is impressive, and the cuisine of quality, with an accent on game dishes. From 900 Kč.

CZECH PUBS

Pivnice U Sv. Tomáše (C E3)
→ Letenská 12
Tel. 257 533 466
Daily noon–11pm
In 1352, Augustinian monks brewed the city's first beer here. These days, Braník (12°), an excellent dark beer, is on offer, as well as *guláš* cooked with beer. Live music in the evening (Thu-Sat).
Dish 120–200 Kč.

U Černého vola (C A4)
→ Loretánské náměstí 1
Tel. 220 513 481
Daily 9am–10pm
A wonderful Czech pub in the heart of the tourist district, the 'Black Bull' is not easy to find but worth the trouble. Once there, confidently make your way through the regulars blocking the entrance, and try to find a vacant space at the back, where a long chest, set against the wall, also acts as a bench.

Velkopopovický Kozel on draft, served to perfection. Very good snacks. Smoky place.

Hostinec Stará radnice (C B4)
→ Loretánská 1
Tel. 220 511 140
Daily 9am–9pm
As said on a blackboard attached to one of the large shutters, the cooking here is 'old-style Bohemian': garlic soup, *guláš*, *apfelstrüdel* and Pilsner Urquell on draft. The service can be brisk. À la carte 250 Kč. Hefty supplement for bread: 150 Kč.

CAFÉS, TEAROOM

U Zavěšeného kafe (C B4)
→ Radnické schody 7 (no tel.) Daily 11am–midnight
This tiny café-gallery, halfway up the steps to the Castle, resembles a cottage. Solid wooden tables occupy most of the two small rooms, adorned with works by Jakub Kreji. The specialty here is the robust *pivní sýr*: cheese with beer, served on a plate with butter, onions, sardines, mustard, paprika and pepper. You have to mix it all together and splash some beer on top

before tucking in.

Kajetánka (C C3)
→ Hradčanské náměstí
Tel. 257 533 735 Daily 10am–6pm (8pm summer)
On the way down from the Castle to the Nerudova. A spiral staircase leads to a small room and a terrace that offers a dizzying view of the red rooftops of Malá Strana. Tea, coffee, beer, wine, soft drinks and modest meals such as *kajetánka* steak (served with cheese and olives).

Malý Buddha (C B4)
→ Úvoz 46 Tel. 220 513 894
Tue-Sun 1pm–10.30pm
As soon as the threshold is crossed, the tone is set: Zen-style music engenders a calm and meditative state – or not, but this is anyway a luminous and healthy meeting spot, creating a positive energy all round. All varieties of herbal teas, Vietnamese cuisine and vegetarian dishes. No smoking.

SHOPPING

Zlatá ulička (C D3)
The 'Golden lane' and its little colored houses seem to come straight out of a fairy tale. Legend has it that in the 18th century the street was home to

'goldmakers', alchemists searching for the secret of the philosopher's stone. Tourists turn up *en masse* to admire the work of the craftsmen who have set up shop here. Beware, prices are astronomical.

N°18: Salónek královny Žofie (C D3)
→ Tel. 224 372 284 Daily 10am–4pm (6pm summer)
Clothes and accessories in natural products.

N°15: Boema (C C3)
→ Tel. 224 372 291
Daily 9am–7pm
Objects created out of blown glass; faithful reproductions of the medieval tradition.

Galerie Benoni (C A3)
→ Thunovská 19
Tel. 257 535 235
Daily 11am–7pm
Pictorial works, with fascinating shapes and perspectives presented by a contemporary school of painting that brilliantly combines creativity and emotions. For amateurs of the avant-garde.

Icons gallery /Antique music instruments (C A4)
→ Pohořelec 9
Tel. 220 514 287
Daily 9am–6pm
This store is stacked high with old musical instruments and icons (with a certificate of authenticity and origin).

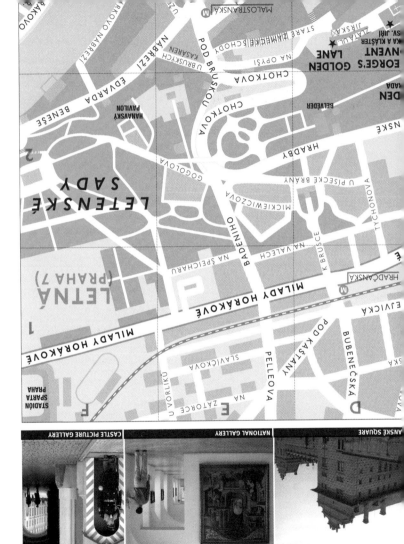

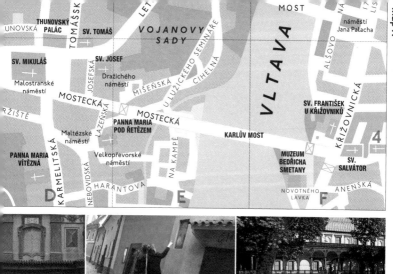

...RGE'S CONVENT | **GOLDEN LANE** | **ROYAL GARDEN**

former stables are ...orks (Tintoretto, ..., Rubens) that have ...ed the dispersion of ...bulous collection of ...ph II (1576–1611).

... Vitus'
...edral (C C3)
...rd courtyard
...4 371 111 Daily
...5pm (4pm Nov-March)
...ggest Gothic church
...country. After the
... of the first architect,
...ew of Arras, in 1344,
...ung Petr Parléř took
...nd experimented with
...chniques for
...ating vaults and ribs.
...signed a chapel over
...mb of the martyred

St Wenceslas (10th century) with walls encrusted with jasper, amethysts and agates. The 21 busts in the triforium are unequalled in Czech sculpture. The construction continued over time, only ending in 1929: a glorious overview of Czech art from the Middle Ages to the 20th century (Art Nouveau stained-glass windows by Mucha).

★ Old Royal Palace (C D3)
→ Third courtyard
Daily 9am–4pm
Although abandoned by the Habsburgs in the 16th century, the palace of the Kings of Bohemia still houses many treasures. The

Vladislav Hall (Benedikt Riel, 1493–1502) occupies the whole upper floor. Its superb vault with intertwined ribbing gives Gothic forms an ornamental treatment, almost qualifying it as baroque.

★ St George's
Convent (C D3)
→ Jiřské náměstí 33
Tel. 257 535 829
Tue-Sun 10am–6pm
The first convent built in Bohemia (937) houses the Czech collections (15th–18th century) of the National Gallery: Mannerist art (Von Aachen, Heinz, Savery), baroque painting and sculpture (Brandl,

Skréta, Braun, Brokof).
★ Golden Lane (C D3)
→ Access from Jiřská
In the 16th century the pretty Liliputian houses clustered around the Castle were no more than humble wooden cabins inhabited by archers, merchants and the gold-beaters that gave the street its name.
★ Royal Garden (C D2)
Big Renaissance garden, planted around 1540 outside the Castle. Superb view of the Castle and the Golden Lane from the garden of the Belvedere, one of the purest examples of Renaissance architecture outside Italy.

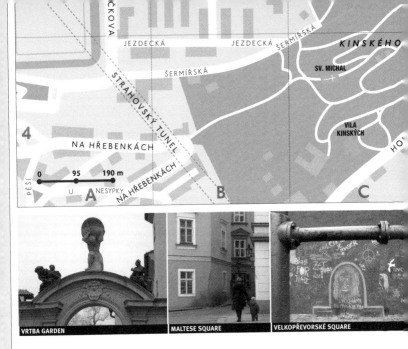

VRTBA GARDEN

MALTESE SQUARE

VELKOPŘEVORSKÉ SQUARE

★ Nerudova (D C1)
The last stretch of the Royal Way clings to the hill and climbs to the Castle, flanked by a series of sublime baroque houses. At n°5, the Morzin Palace (Santini-Aichi, 1713) and its evocative balcony, borne by caryatids sculpted by Brokof. At n°20, the Thun-Hohenstein Palace (1713) and its portal adorned with two eagles (Braun). At n°47, the house of the essayist and poet Jan Neruda (1834–91). Above the front doors, old shop signs ('At the 3 violins', 'At the Golden Cup') provide touching reminders of the trades of the houses' former inhabitants.

★ St Thomas' Church (D D1)
→ *Josefská 8*
Tel. 257 530 556 Open during religious services
The extremely narrow Josef street is overwhelmed by the sculptural baroque façade of this church (K. I. Dientzenhofer, 1723–31). Golden Corinthian capitals, stuccos, moldings, vaults painted with frescos (Václav Reiner, 1728–30) contrast with the soaring nave, which recalls the Gothic origins of the church, founded by Augustinians (1285–1379).

★ Wallenstein Palace (D D1)
→ *Letenská 10*
Garden: April-Oct, daily 10am–6pm
Elegant late-Renaissance palace, built between 1623 and 1629 for the Duke of Wallenstein. Facing the baroque gardens (open to the public) is the Sala Terrena, big Italian-style loggia, the masterpiece of the Mannerist Giovanni Pieroni.

★ Malá Strana Square (D D1)
→ *Malostranské náměstí*
The heart of Malá Strana. The huge, gently sloping square, centered on

St Nicholas' Church, boasts an almost thea[..] diversity: Renaissance alongside baroque, bourgeois houses nex[..] arches built after the 1[..] fire. The focus of the u[..] part of the Malostrans[..] is on the neoclassical Liechtenstein Palace (°

★ St Nicholas' Church (D D1)
→ *Malostranské náměs[..]*
Tel. 257 534 215 Daily 9am–5pm (4pm Nov-M[..]
The spiritual strongho[..] the Counter-Reformati[..] this is also the crowni[..] glory of Prague's baro[..] style (Dientzenhofer fa[..] and son, 1703–55). Th[..]

D

map 2

BREVNOV

PETŘÍN

SEMINÁŘ ZAHRA

M STR (PRA

SV. VAVŘINEC

VANICKOVA

STRAHOVSKA

STRAHOVSKA ZAHRADA

LOBKOVICKA ZAHRADA

STRAHOV (PRAHA 1)

2

VRTBA GAR
VRTBOVSKÁ ZAHRADA

LOBKOVICKÝ PALÁC

VLAŠSKÁ

Strahovské nádvoří

NEMOCNICE MILOSRDNÝCH SESTER

SV. KAREL BOROMEJSKÝ

STRAHOVSKÝ KLÁŠTER

SV. ROCH

VLAŠSKÁ

VRÁSEK BŘETISLA

JANSKÝ

POHOŘELEC

MORZIN PAL

NERUDOVA

ÚVOZ

SV. KAJETAN

NERUD

SCHWARZENBERSKÝ PALÁC

RADNICKÉ SCHODY

TOSKÁNSKÝ PALÁC

LORETÁNSKÁ

Loretánské náměstí

KATED SV. V

ZÁMISL

Hradčanské náměstí

U KASÁREN

LORETA

KAPUCÍNSKÁ

PANNA MARIA ANDĚLSKÁ

KEPLEROVA

ARCIBISKUPSKÝ PALÁC

SV. JAN NEPOMUCKY

ČERNÍNSKÁ

ČERNÍNSKÝ PALÁC

C

OBRAZÁRNA PRAŽSKÉHO HRADU (NÁRODNÍ GALERIE)

ŠTERNBERSKÝ PALÁC (NÁRODNÍ GALERIE)

B

KANOVNICKÁ

U BRUSNICE

NOVÝ SVĚT

A

NERUDOVA STREET

ST THOMAS' CHURCH

WALLENSTEIN PALACE

Malá Strana

Nestled under Petřín Hill, Malá Strana (the 'Little Quarter') slopes down from Hradčany to the Vltava in a cascade of red roofs, which are interspersed with lush gardens and vineyards. In Malá Strana there has barely been a new building since the 18th century, and the whole area, with its medieval layout of alleys, passageways, steps, and cul-de-sacs, is ideal for strolling. Its baroque palaces try to outshine each other with statues and hidden gardens. A cable car ride leads to the top of the hill and the Belvedere, with a tiny replica of the Eiffel tower. In this romantic spot, time stands still as the Vltava casts its hypnotic spell....

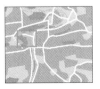

CANTINA

RESTAURANTS

Bohemia Bagel (D D3)
→ *Újezd 16*
Tel. 257 310 694
Daily 8am–midnight
Delicious bagels, toasted on request, plain or in various flavors (sesame, garlic or onion), filled with salmon and cream cheese, chili. But also: soups, sandwiches, quiches and salads. An unlimited supply of coffee and soft drinks. Home deliveries. Non-smoking area. Bagel 65–90 Kč.

Čertovká (D E1)
→ *U Lužického semináře 24*
Tel. 257 532 205
Daily 11.30am–10pm
Wonderful terrace by the Vltava. The place is usually full of tourists, but the view over Charles Bridge is stunning. Czech and international cuisine. Access by boat. À la carte 300–400 Kč.

Cantina (D D3)
→ *Újezd 38*
Tel. 257 317 173
Daily noon–11pm
Homesick American expats have found their diner, and it has caught on with the locals too. Good Tex-Mex cooking (chili, *burritos*, *fajitas*). Cocktails (mojito, piña colada) 100 Kč. À la carte 400 Kč.

U sedmi Švábů (D C1)
→ *Jánský vršek 14*
Tel. 257 531 455
Daily 11am–10pm
In winter, when the cold is merciless, sitting by the fireplace is heaven. This 'medieval' tavern (oil lamps, waiters in costume) serves dishes based on recipes from the 15th and 16th century. All the ingredients are exclusively from that period (so no potatoes as they were still unknown in Europe). Goose liver with almonds, carp with garlic, roast beef with apples and blueberries. Menu: 555 Kč. Special 'Eat-as-much-as-you-like' menu... 1,300 Kč.

Nebozízek (D C3)
→ *Petřínské sady 411*
Tel. 257 315 329
Daily 11am–11pm
The incredible location of Nebodízek, on the slopes of Petřín Hill, attracts many tourists but also a considerable number of locals when their plan is a special night out. As a meeting place for a romantic dinner, Nebodízek is hard to beat. The cuisine is good (international, with Czech specialties such as roast

IOLAS CAFÉ | **ZANZI BAR** | **GALERIE MARRIONETTA**

pork, garlic soup), but what you come for are the fantastic views over the city. The restaurant is reached via the Petřín cable car (get off at the Nebozízek stop). Reserve ahead if you want one of the best window tables. À la carte 650 Kč.

Pasha (D E1)

→ U Lužického semináře 23
Tel. 257 532 434
www.pasha.cz
Daily 11.30am–11pm
Warm, inviting restaurant with an interior in hues of blue and red, fine beamed ceiling, carpets. Very attentive service and delicious Turkish and Lebanese cuisine – a winning combination. Dish 350 Kč.

Bazaar Mediterranee (D C1)

→ Nerudova 40
Tel. 257 535 050
Restaurant: daily noon–11pm;
Bar: daily 10pm–2am
Excellent restaurant with a Mediterranean touch (salmon with truffles and fresh pasta, gazpacho, Moroccan kefta, bouillabaisse). Lively atmosphere, too, with drag show, parades of go-go girls, live music... In summer, dine in the garden or on the terrace

overlooking the city. À la carte 1,000 Kč.

U modré kachničky (D D2)

→ Nebovidská 6
Tel. 257 320 308
Daily noon–4pm, 6.30–11.30pm
The 'Blue Duckling' has it all: sumptuous retro setting (vaults painted with frescos, 19th-century furniture, floral fabrics) and a menu paying tribute to the splendor of Bohemian cuisine. Delicious starters (roe deer paté), game specialties (wild duck, pheasant, wild boar, venison), and traditional Czech dishes such as an outstanding guláš. Another branch in Staré Město at Michalská 16. À la carte 1,200 Kč.

CAFÉ

St Nicholas Café (D D2)

→ Tržiště 10
Tel. 257 530 204
Mon-Fri noon–1am (2am Fri); Sat-Sun 4pm–1am (2am Sat)
A quiet spot in the heart of the tourist district, ideal for meeting for a drink or something more substantial, such as pork with potato croquettes.

BARS, MUSIC VENUES

Zanzi Bar (D D2)

→ Lázeňská 6
Tel. 0602 286 657
Daily 5pm–3am
The chic headquarters of young locals and foreign students who come to be seen, but also to enjoy the endless drinks list: 76 cocktails (including an explosive mixture with absinthe). Fine selection of Cuban cigars. Concerts (rock, jazz, blues) several times a month.

U malého Glena (D D2)

→ Karmelitská 23
Tel. 257 531 717
Daily 10am–2am
Have a snack on the ground floor (soups, sandwiches) before going down to the tiny, usually packed, vaulted hall (come early if you want a seat). A keen and cheerful crowd of thirty-somethings listens to jazz, acid jazz and Bohemian blues. Jam session on Sundays. Seven types of beer, Irish (Guinness, Murphy's) and Czech (Pilsner Urquell, Staro-pramen, Kelt, Velvet).

Malostranská Beseda (D D2)

→ Malostranské náměstí 21
(entrance under arcades)

Tel. 257 532 092
Daily 8.30pm–1am
The bar opens at 5pm for ticket holders. Concerts every night, by Czech or foreign groups (rock, jazz, country).

SHOPPING

Galerie Marrionetta (D E1)

→ U Lužického semináře 7
Tel. 257 535 091
Daily 10am–6pm
The clowns and goblins in the window sneer at passers-by with their creepy grimaces. The puppet tradition goes back to the 17th century and the Czechs are past masters of this art. It has given birth to vivid stock characters: the duo Špejbl and Hurvínek (father and son), Kašparek (clown), the witch, Death, the Devil and other mysterious figures from a dark, enchanted world.

Galerie Peron (D E1)

→ U Lužického semináře 12
Tel. 257 533 507
Mon-Fri 11–7pm; Sat-Sun noon–6pm; www.peron.cz
Design pieces and artworks from the 1960s to the present day. The gallery holds regular exhibitions.

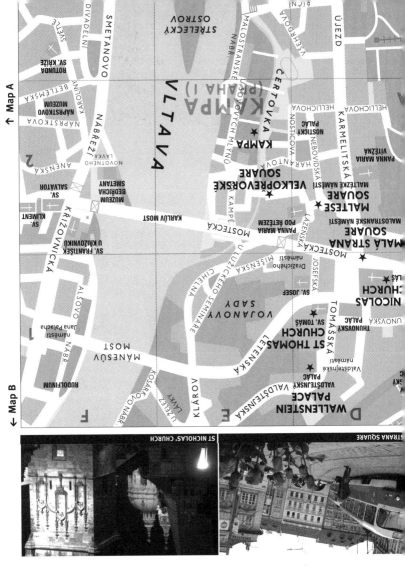

ST NICHOLAS, CHURCH

STRANA SQUARE

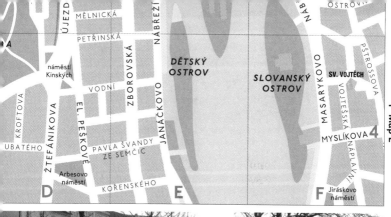

PETŘÍN HILL

ing church has an
ngly light touch and
ates the square
ut being
owering. Curving
es, dilated vaults, a
e-catching cupola:
ect osmosis between
chitectural lines and
ulent rococo decor.
os imitating marble
urving trompe-l'œil
ngs give the whole
ure an astonishing
of movement.

ba Garden (D C2)
melitská 18
7 531 480
ct: daily 10am–6pm
5 Karmelitská street,
d a courtyard, is one

of the most resplendent
terraced baroque gardens in
Prague (F. M. Kanka, 1720).
The loggia is decorated with
statues from Brokof's
workshop. Wonderful view
of Malá Strana and the city
stretching behind it.

★ **Kampa (D** E2)
Intimate, sheltered from the
hubbub of the city, Kampa
Island seems enchanted. It
is linked to Malá Strana via
the little bridges straddling
the Devil's Stream, which
was once flanked by
windmills. On a stroll round
its alleys, details grab the
eye – a rococo adornment
here, a balcony rail there –
only adding to the overall

charm. Its glorious park
offers a superb view of
Charles Bridge and the
opposite bank of the Vltava.
★ **Maltese Square (D** D2)
→ *Maltézské náměstí*
This L-shaped square,
untouched by time,
bounded by elegant
baroque and rococo houses
was the dream setting for
Miloš Forman's movie
Amadeus. To the south,
the Nostitz Palace,
attributed to Caratti.
★ **Velkopřevorské
Square (D** E2)
A powerful symbol of
dissidence lovingly
preserved: opposite the
imposing baroque portal

of the Buquoy Palace, a
wall covered with graffiti,
including a portrait of
John Lennon.
★ **Petřín Hill (D** C3)
→ *Petřínské sady (access
via cable car from Újezd)*
On the top, the Belvedere,
and a miniature Eiffel Tower
built in 1891 for the
Universal Exhibition.
Nestling in greenery, the
baroque St Lawrence's
Church (1735–70) set into
the Wall of Hunger built by
Charles IV to provide work
for the poor. Further south,
the Kinský Gardens and
the old Orthodox sanctuary
of St Michael of Petřín
(18th century).

WENCESLAS SQUARE

SLAV ISLAND

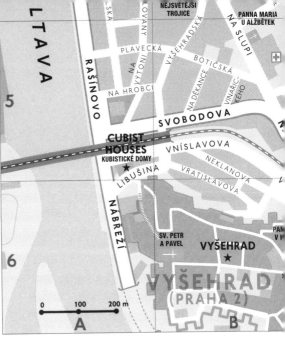

NEJSVĚTĚJŠÍ TROJICE

PANNA MARIA U ALŽBĚTEK

PLAVECKÁ

SVOBODOVA

BOTIČSKÁ

VNÍSLAVOVA

CUBIST HOUSES
KUBISTICKÉ DOMY

LIBUŠINA

NEKLANOVA

VRATISLAVOVA

NÁBŘEŽÍ

SV. PETR A PAVEL

VYŠEHRAD

VYŠEHRAD (PRAHA 2)

0   100   200 m

A   B

★ Rotunda of the Holy Cross (E A1)

→ Konviktská/Karoliny

One of the last gems of Romanesque Prague (12th century). A small chapel with a conical roof, characteristic of the style of the Přemyslids kings (11th-14th centuries). Inside, the remains of Gothic murals (14th century).

★ Národní (E A1)

One of the city's liveliest streets, laid in 1871 along the ramparts of the Old Town. At the beginning of the 20th century, the avenue became the favorite strolling ground of the local bourgeoisie. It has preserved its famous cafés, its theaters and its belle-époque architectural treasures. Two adjoining buildings by Osvald Polívka reflect the different tendencies of Czech Art Nouveau. At n° 9, the Topič House (1910) is similar to the Germanic Jugendstil; at n° 7, the more abstract former Praha Insurance Company Building (1905–07) was influenced by the Viennese Sezession.

★ Church of Our Lady of the Snows (E C1)

→ Jungmannovo náměstí 18
Tel. 224 490 349
Open for religious services
Commissioned by Charles IV in 1347 to stage his coronation, this would have been Prague's biggest building. However, only the choir was ever finished as religious wars prevented its total completion. Nevertheless, it is still the city's second biggest Gothic church, after the cathedral. Lovely adjacent garden.

★ Wenceslas Square (E C1)

Demonstrations against Nazism (1938), the Liberation celebrations (1945), haranguing of Soviet tanks (1968), Jan Palach setting fire to himself (1969) in protest against the repression of the Prague Spring... Twenty years later, the square became the stage for the popular of the Velvet Revolutio hastened the downfa the Communist regim The heart of the New (2,460 feet long) belo the people!

★ Slav Island / Mánes Gallery (E A

→ Masarykovo nábřež
Tel. 224 930 754
Tue-Sun 10am–6pm
The Functionalist buil of the Mánes Gallery (Otakar Novotný, 193 links the Masaryk Qua the southern-most po Slav Island. It incorpo the Renaissance towe one of the four water

E

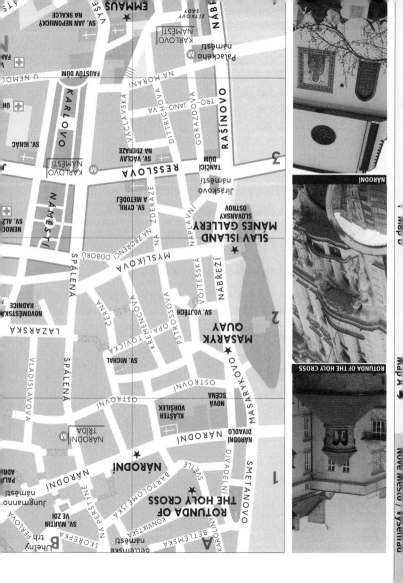

ROTUNDA OF THE HOLY CROSS

NÁRODNÍ

Nové Město / Vyšehrad

Wide avenues, elegant hundred-year-old galleries, monumental squares: the 'New Town', born of a 14th-century planning project, revolves around the enormous Wenceslas Square, once the focus of Czech opposition to the Soviet occupation. Na příkopě and Národní teem with restaurants, cafés and stores. To the south of Nové Město lies the legendary cradle of the princes of Bohemia, the 'other' castle, perched on Vyšehrad Hill and overlooking the Vltava. You can reach it by walking up Vratislava street and, as with many other places in Prague, the visit is a magical trip back in time, far from the bustle of the center. At the foot of the hill are Josef Chochol's Cubist buildings.

CAFÉ SLAVIA

CAFÉ PATIO

RESTAURANTS

Dynamo (E A2)
→ Pštrossova 220/29
Tel. 224 932 020
Daily 11.30am–11pm
The hip designer furniture and minimalist decor is in keeping with the spirit of Dynamo's young clientele. The restaurant offers a simple menu – salads, grilled meats and big plates of pasta (dishes around 100 Kč), but you can simply sit at the bar, trying one of the 90 whiskies on offer. À la carte 400 Kč.

Le Bistrot de Marlène (E A5)
→ Plavecká 4
Tel. 224 921 853
Mon–Fri noon–2.30pm, 7–10.30pm; Sat 7–10.30pm
Since 1995 Marlène Salomon has regaled her customers (both locals and tourists) with the simple but refined and generous French cooking influenced by the 15 years she'd previously spent in Provence. The key to her success: the consistently fresh ingredients, which vary according to the season. Veal medallion with tarragon, goat's cheese salad with pesto, pheasant terrine and foie gras... À la carte 1,000 Kč.

La Perle de Prague (E A3)
→ Rašínovo nábřeží 80
Tel. 221 984 160
Mon 7–10.30pm; Tue–Sat noon–2pm, 7–10.30pm; Bar: 9am–2am
On the seventh floor of the 'dancing house', the unusual and controversial 1996 building by the Californian architect Frank Gehry. Top-class French cuisine, but perhaps not as spectacular as the views of the Vltava, the Castle and Petřín Hill. Terrace in summer. À la carte 1,800 Kč (lunch menu 900 Kč).

CZECH PUBS

U pinkasů (E B1)
→ Jungmannovo náměstí 15/16. Tel. 224 222 965
Daily 9am–11pm
One of the few taverns in the city that has retained its authenticity. Smoky vibe, clinking tankards, regulars leaning on the bar. Pilsner Urquell has been sold here on draft since 1843.

U Fleků (E A2)
→ Kremenkova 11
Tel. 224 934 465
Daily 9am–11pm
A favorite with tourists, this pub is really worth a visit for the 15th-century building housing it, but also for the very good beer brewed on the premises.

KORUNA PALÁC

LUCERNA PASÁŽ

CAFÉS, TEAROOM

Café Patio (E B1)
→ Národní 22
Tel. 224 934 375
Mon–Fri 8am–11pm;
Sat–Sun 10am–11pm
Store: Tel. 224 934 402
Mon–Sat 10am–7pm;
Sun 11am–7pm
Redbrick walls, dark
wooden furniture,
wrought-iron lamps – the
bric-à-brac decor
creates a very laid-back
mood. Good choice of
cafés, snacks and
pastries. Store in the
basement selling
wrought-iron pieces,
chandeliers, etc.

Café Slavia (E A1)
→ Smetanovo 2
Tel. 224 218 493
Daily 8am–11pm
Smetana, Dvořák, Havel:
ever since 1863 writers,
musicians and dissident
intellectuals have
occupied the benches of
this legendary café, which
was the last palace built
for an aristocrat, Count
Lazansky. The closure of
this former bastion of
dissent in 1992 aroused
protests from President
Havel, among others. The
Slavia finally reopened in
1998, with the addition of
a wonderful restaurant.
Its 'absinthe-green' Art
Deco interior still has a
magnetic appeal to an
eclectic crowd of tourists,
businessmen and old
Czech ladies. Have tea
with pastries and revel in
the wonderful ambience.
Big bay windows opening
out onto the river. Enter
via Národní.

Café Louvre (E B1)
→ Národní 20
Tel. 224 930 949
Daily 9am–midnight
Another of Prague's
elegant cafés, where
Franz Kafka and Max
Brod used to meet. On
the first floor are three
bright, spacious rooms.
Coffee, tea, pastries,
meals, all served with
style by waiters in white
aprons.

Dobrá čajovna (E C1)
→ Václavské náměstí 14
Tel. 224 231 480
Mon–Sat 10am–9.30pm;
Sun 2–9.30pm
A retreat from the bustle
of Wenceslas Square. This
tearoom stocks a variety
of teas (China, Taiwan,
Japan, Africa) that can
also be purchased.

BARS, JAZZ CLUB,
MUSIC VENUE

Reduta (E B1)
→ Národní 20
Tel. 224 933 487 Daily 9pm
(concerts 9.30pm)
Founded in 1958, this is
one of Prague's great jazz
institutions. Regular
sessions are held here.

Velryba (E A2)
→ Opatovická 24
Tel. 224 932 391
Daily 11am–midnight
Opened in 1989, 'the
whale' was the city's first
café-gallery. At lunchtime,
students and young
artists come to read a
newspaper over a coffee
or a plate of pasta. At
night, alcohol and
tobacco take over. The
second room provides
more intimacy. Gallery in
the basement. Gambrinus
(bottle) and strong liquor.

Rock Café (E B1)
→ Národní 20
Tel. 224 933 947
www.rockcafe.cz
Mon–Fri 10am–3am;
Sat–Sun 5pm–3am (1am
Sun). Concerts: daily 8.30pm
One of the pioneers of
underground rock, the
Rock Café has gone on
to greater things. Concert
hall, movie theater, CD
store, Internet corner. It
remains pretty deserted
during the day.

**Lucerna
Music Bar (E** C1)
→ Vodičkova 36
Tel. 224 217 108
Coffeeshop: daily 11am–
5pm. Bar daily 8pm–3am
Concerts: 9pm
In a basement, on two
levels, are a bar and a
concert hall, where the
best local and sometimes
international groups come
to play an eclectic
program of 1960s rock,
disco, blues, reggae and
jazz. The hall is hired out
every October by the
Prague Jazz Festival.

SHOPPING

Koruna Palác (E C1)
→ Václavské náměstí
(corner Na příkopě)
Tel. 224 219 526
Daily 9am–8pm
Shopping mall in a
beautiful Jugendstil
building, with Bonton,
the biggest record store
in town, set up in the
basement.

Lucerna pasáž (E C1)
Magnificent shopping
passageway (1912–16),
built by Václav Havel's
grandfather.

Galery Mody
→ Štěpánská 61
Tel. 224 211 514
Daily 10am–7pm
On the first floor of the
passage, Mody sells
clothes by Czech
designers like Helena
Fejková (linen clothes).
Small café at the entrance.

CUBIST HOUSES

VYŠEHRAD

its that once supplied
y's public fountains.
mporary art
tion. Pleasant strolls
/ Island Park.

■saryk Quay (E A2)
Karlovu, 20
ful collection of neo-
ssance, neo-baroque
t Nouveau buildings.
t miss n° 32, with
ely entrance on the
' of the Goethe
te (Jiri Stibral 1904–
markable stuccos by
Klouček at n° 26.

ořák Museum (E C3)
Karlovu, 20
4 923 363
'n 10am–5pm
nerika Villa, an
t baroque house by

Kilián Ignác Dientzenhofer
(1720), has contained the
Dvořák Museum since 1932.
Original scores, letters,
former possessions of the
famous composer, born to
the north of Prague in
Nelahozeves.

**★ Emmaus Convent/
St John-Nepomuk-on-the-
Rock (E** B4)
→ *Vyšehradská 49*
Tel. 224 915 371
Severely tested by the
Hussite wars (1420), the
sanctuaries now only show
a few traces of their Gothic
murals. The fragments of
frescos (14th century) kept
in the cloister of Emmaus
Convent are some of the

most exquisite in Bohemia.
Just opposite, perched on a
rock, a tiny church devoted
to St John Nepomuk, one
of the treasures of baroque
art (K. I. Dientzenhofer,
1730–49).

★ Cubist houses (E A5)
→ *Neklanova 30/Libušina 3/
Rašínovo nábřeží 6-8-10*
Prague is the only city in the
world to have developed
this type of architecture.
Several examples on the
foot of Vyšehrad Hill by
Josef Chochol (1880–1956).
Masterpiece: the Kovařovič
villa (Libušina 3), built on
a triangular site in 1913.
Spectacular corner pillar
on the apartment building

(Neklanova 30) situated at
the junction of two streets.

★ Vyšehrad (E B6)
Legend has it that Princess
Libuše built Prague Castle
on Vyšehrad Hill in 717 after
having a vision. She chose
a husband by the name of
Přemysl, and they started
the Přemyslid dynasty
(which lasted until 1306).
Vyšehrad became the
stronghold of the first kings
of Bohemia, although it was
later replaced by Hradčany.
Stunning views from the
park and the ramparts of
the fortress. Some of the
nation's greatest artists
(Smetana, Dvořák, Mucha)
rest in the cemetery (1870).

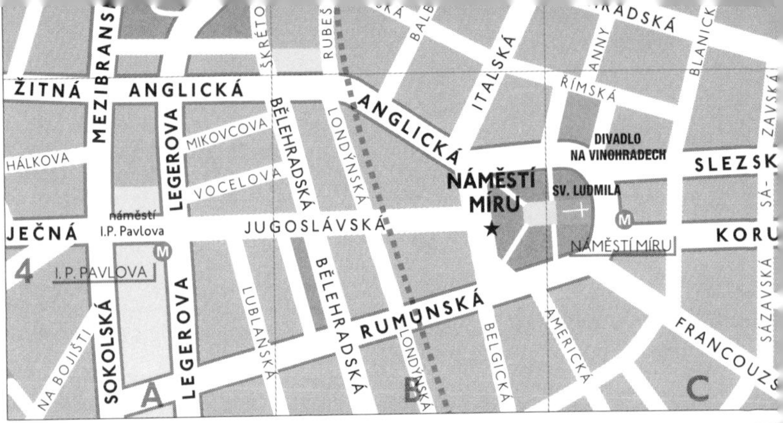

Map labels: ŽITNÁ, ANGLICKÁ, MEZIBRANSKÁ, BRANSKÁ, ŠKRÉTOVA, RUBEŠ, BALB, BALE, RADSKÁ, BLANICK, ANNY, HÁLKOVA, LEGEROVA, MIKOVCOVA, BĚLEHRADSKÁ, LONDÝNSKÁ, ANGLICKÁ, ITALSKÁ, ŘÍMSKÁ, IMSKA, ZAVSK, DIVADLO NA VINOHRADECH, SLEZSK, VOCELOVA, NÁMĚSTÍ MÍRU, SV. LUDMILA, JEČNÁ, náměstí I.P. Pavlova, JUGOSLÁVSKÁ, BĚLEHRADSKÁ, NÁMĚSTÍ MÍRU, KORU, I. P. PAVLOVA, SA, LUBLANSKÁ, SOKOLSKÁ, LEGEROVA, BĚLEHRADSKÁ, RUMUNSKÁ, LONDÝNSKÁ, BELGICKÁ, AMERICKÁ, FRANCOUZ, SAZAVSKA, NA BOJIŠTI, LUBLANSKÁ, C

SECESSION HOUSE, MÁNESOVA

SECESSION HOUSES, VINHORADSKÁ

★ Mucha Museum (F A2)
→ Panská 7
Tel. 221 451 333
Daily 10am–6pm
The life and work of the most widely known Czech artist. In 1895, Alfons Mucha (1860–1939) became famous through a poster he designed for a Sarah Bernhardt theater play, and set off for Paris, where he launched the Art Nouveau style: floral and vegetal motifs, female figures with endlessly flowing hair. Back in Prague in 1910, he helped decorate the Town Hall and then designed the stained-glass windows for St Vitus'

Cathedral. His last work was the *Slav Epic*, a cycle of 20 enormous paintings. The 5,400 square feet of floor space embrace the various facets of Mucha's talent (posters, decorative panels, pastels, paintings, drawings, sketches). Store (sale of reproductions).

★ Central Station (F B2)
→ Hlavní nádraží / Wilsonová 8
The city's largest building in the Secession style (1901–09), after the Town Hall. Josef Fanta (1856–1954) let his imagination run wild, with colors and ornamental details tumbling over each other,

especially in the semi-circular dome.

★ State Opera (F B3)
→ Wilsonová 84
Tel. 224 227 266 (bookings)
Mon–Fri 10am–5.30pm; Sat–Sun 10am–noon, 1–5.30pm
Spurred on by the monumental National Theater whose foundation stone was laid in 1868, Prague's German community commissioned two Austrian architects to build a 'German theater'. In 1888 this exact, though smaller, copy of the Vienna Opera House (and of Prague's biggest theaters) opened, staging operas by Strauss and symphonies

by Mahler. Today it als shows foreign operas.

★ National Museum (F A3)
→ Václavské náměstí 6
Tel. 224 497 111
Daily 10am–6pm (9am–5pm winter)
Founded in 1918 durin wave of Czech patrioti like the National Thea the Museum embodie the nationalist revival contains precious me documents (library), s and meteorites (grour floor), collections of C minerals, zoology and paleontology (first flo

★ Náměstí Míru (F
The layout of the Peac

F

NATIONAL MUSEUM

STATE OPERA — STÁTNÍ OPERA

NA SMETANCE

ITALSKÁ

HELENSKÁ

ŠPANĚLSKÁ

LICHNICKÁ

KUNĚTICKÁ

ŽELEZNIČNÍ NEMOCNICE

ITALSKÁ

WASHINGTONOVA

OPLETALOVA

WILSONOVA

Václavské náměstí

MUZEUM

CENTRAL STATION
PRAHA-HLAVNÍ NÁDRAŽÍ

HLAVNÍ NÁDRAŽÍ

VRCHLICKÉHO SADY

OPLETALOVA

OPLETALOVA

OPLETALOVA

OLIVOVA

RŮŽOVA

JINDŘIŠSKÁ

PANSKÁ

U PŮJČOVNY

PRAHA-MASARYKOVO NÁDRAŽÍ

JERUZALÉMSKÁ

SV. JINDŘICH A KUNHUTA

MUCHOVO MUZEUM

MUCHA MUSEUM

JUBILEJNÍ SYN.

Senovážné náměstí

BOLZANOVA

DLÁŽDĚNÁ

SENOVÁŽNÁ

POŠTA

MUZEUM POLITICKÝCH VĚZŇŮ

WILSONOVA

PŘÍBĚN

HUSIT

HYBERNSKÁ

HAVLÍČKOVA

PRAHA-MASARYKOVO NÁDRAŽÍ

PRAHA-FLORENC
AUTOBUSOVÉ NÁDRAŽÍ

V CELNICI

NÁMĚSTÍ REPUBLIKY

náměstí Republiky

OBECNÍ DŮM

PRAŠNÁ BRÁNA

MUCHA MUSEUM

CENTRAL STATION

STATE OPERA

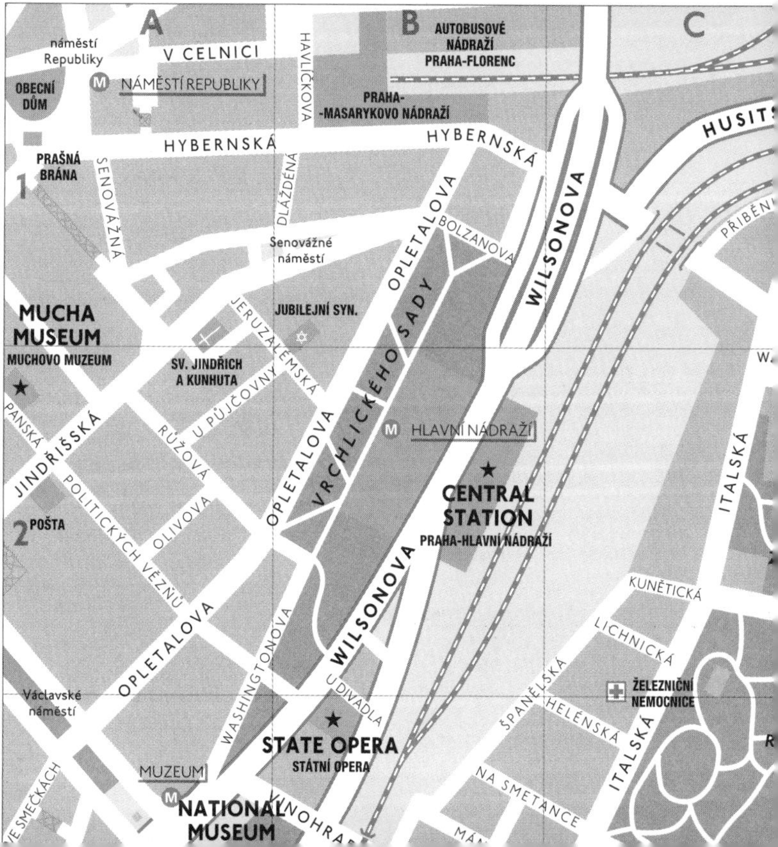

A

B

C

1

2

Big parks, tree-lined avenues, sophisticated Secession and Art Nouveau buildings: the former royal vineyards of Vinohrady, planted by Charles IV in the 14th century, were built up at the end of the 19th century to provide residences for the Czech bourgeoisie. Vinohrady is now mutating again, and becoming less residential in the process, as some of the city's most select bars and nightclubs have opened here to attract the local trendsetters. Further to the east lies Žižkov (named after the Hussite chief Jan Žižka). The concrete houses of this old working-class stronghold are now venues for a growing alternative scene.

TOWER PRAHA RESTAURANT

KAVÁRNA MEDÚZA

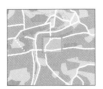

RESTAURANTS

Pizzeria Grosseto (F C4)
→ *Francouzká 2*
Tel. 224 252 778
www.grosseto.cz
Daily 11.30am–11pm
Third restaurant opened by the same Italian owner in Prague. The pizzas cooked to perfection, the fresh, tasty salads, and desserts such as zabaglione and tiramisù have made this pizzeria extremely popular. Plus, it's good value for money. Pizza 80–150 Kč.

Ambiente (F D3)
→ *Mánesova 59*
Tel. 222 727 851
Mon-Fri 11am–11.30pm; Sat-Sun 1–11.30pm
Part of a chain in the Czech Republic, Ambiente specializes in Sunny decor and a mix of North American-style food with a Mediterranean twist: corn on the cob, quesadillas and ten different types of fresh pasta. Save room for dessert. Very popular, it is often full, so it is worth reserving a table. À la carte 400 Kč.

Tower Praha restaurant (F E2)
→ *Mahlerovy sady 1*
Tel. 267 005 766 /788
Daily 11am–11pm
Reserve a table 100 feet above town, at the top of the television tower and dine with a breathtaking view of the Vinohrady and Žižkov neighborhoods. Average international cuisine – carpaccio, chicken soup with shallots and almonds, pancakes, grilled fish and meat. À la carte 300 Kč.

Ponte (F B4)
→ *Anglická 15*
Tel. 224 221 665
Mon-Sat 11.30am–11pm
www.ponte-restaurant.cz
Elegant restaurant, with international cuisine and Czech specialties such as *svíčková na smetaně* (roast beef with cream and blueberries). In winter, try to find a spot near the fireplace. There is a wide range of cocktails and a good wine list. À la carte 700 Kč.

CZECH PUB

U Vystřelenýho oka (F E1)
→ *U Božích Bojovníků 3*
Tel. 222 540 465
Mon-Sat 4.30pm–1am
A tavern at the end of a cul-de-sac in the Žižkov neighborhood. Its name, which translates as the

ČENÁ HUSA

FX RADOST

PAVILÓN

'shot eye', refers to a famous one-eyed Hussite chieftain. The mural by Martin Velisek also humorously evokes the Hussite era. Mixed local clientele. Radegast and Velkopopovický on draft, to accompany *utopenec* (Czech sausage and onion marinated in vinegar). Good selection of spirits and wines.

CAFÉS

Spika Internet Café (F B1)
→ Dlážděná 4
Tel. 224 211 521
www.netcafe.spika.cz
Daily 8am–midnight
Art Nouveau interior and state-of-the-art equipment in this cyber-café. From 20 Kč/15 mins.

Potrefená Husa (F F3)
→ Vinohradská 104 and Kolínská 19
Tel. 267 310 360
Daily 11.30am–1am
A red ceiling, a stadium-like concrete vault and six TV screens above the bar. A sporty decor for one of Prague's most agreeable cafés, dedicated to one thing (apart from sport): drinking beer. The service is discreet and friendly and customers can spend

hours here nursing one pint between their hands without being made to feel ill at ease. Staropramen, Velvet, Kelt on draft. Plus snacks such as homemade soups, grills and salads.

Kavárna Medúza (F B4)
→ Belgická 17
Tel. 222 515 107
Mon–Fri 11am–1am;
With old photos on the walls, comfortable armchairs that are conducive to long stays, gentle music (classical or cabaret) in the background, this café has become a neighborhood institution. Salads, sandwiches, a wide variety of generously served drinks and coffees (Viennese, Irish, Algerian) and a host of cocktails.

BARS, JAZZ CLUB, NIGHTCLUBS

U sedmi vlků (F E2)
→ Vlkova 7
Summer: daily 6pm–midnight.
Winter: daily 7–11pm
'At the seven wolves' is an inviting café-bar that draws a young and equally relaxed clientele. Small-scale concerts and DJ sessions in the basement.

Agharta (F A3)
→ Krakovská 5
Tel. 222 211 275
www.agharta.cz
Sun–Thu 5pm–midnight (7pm Fri–Sat); Bar: daily 9am–7pm (concerts 9pm)
This club, founded in 1991, is for true jazz lovers. Foreign and Czech musicians (e.g. Jiří Stívin , flute, Karel Růžička sax) play here. Warm, intimate setting. Jazz CDs on sale at the door.

Palác Akropolis (F E2)
→ Kubelíkova 27
Tel. 296 330 911
www.palacakropolis.cz
A hip alternative cultural center in an old movie theater. It has a café, two bars, a concert hall and stages theater shows, indie rock and world music concerts.
Akropolis Café
→ Mon–Fri 10am–midnight; Sat–sun 4pm–midnight
A tiny café at the back of the hall provides an intimate space. Velvet on draft, cocktails (such as the very strong Becherovka and tonic).
Divadelní bar / Mala scena
→ Daily 7pm–3am/4am
Bar open from 7pm and, every night, from 11pm, DJs rock the joint. A lot of

people come here to be seen. Often packed.
FX radost (F B4)
→ Bělehradská 120
Tel. 224 254 776
www.radostfx.cz
Café + bar: daily 11am–4m
Club: Thu–Sat 10pm–5am
The reputation of Prague's trendiest techno-house club has gone international. The wordly clientele mainly comprises fashion models, young Czech go-getters and Anglo-Saxon dandies, all adept at the art of clubbing, perfectly at ease with the slick decor. It may be difficult for non-members of the tribe to get in. Vegetarian restaurant upstairs.

SHOPPING

Pavilón (F D4)
→ Vinohradská 50
Tel. 222 097 111
Mon–Sat 9.30am–9pm;
Sun noon–8pm
The old covered market – which is situated in a magnificent neo-baroque building with a metal structure – has been converted into a shopping arcade. Major Western brands but also an Italian café and a big grocery store in the basement.

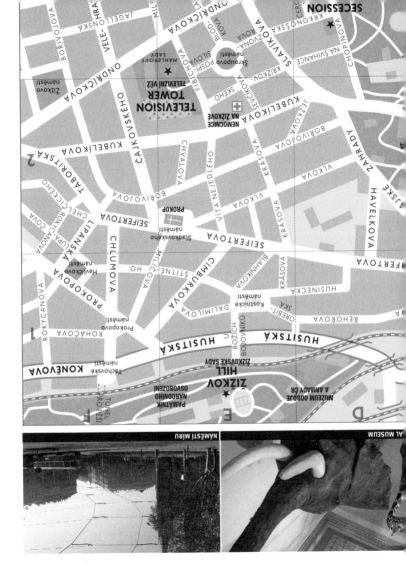

OF THE SACRED HEART | TELEVISION TOWER | ŽIŽKOV HILL

e reflects a
chical approach to
planning, organized
d a space containing
nohrady Theater
-07), a neo-baroque
ng with Art Nouveau
ation; and the neo-
. Church of Saint
la (1888–93). The
served as a meeting
during the Velvet
ution, and its two
onal 194-foot-high
can be seen for
around.

cession

es (F D3)
nesova / Chopinova /
hance / Krkonišská
n architectural stroll

between Mánesova and the
eastern side of Riegrovy
Park to discover the
Secession style.
Ornamentation rules, and
it is integrated into the
buildings' very structures.
At n° 4 on Chopinova,
the Jan Kotěra House
(1908–09): imposing
bow-window and daring
redbrick decoration. At
n° 6, the Bohumil Waigant
House (1909–10): angular
architecture marking
the transition to the
geometrical phase of the
Secession style. At n° 3
on Na Švihance, the
L. Čapek House (1907–08):
remarkable bow window.

Beautiful views of the city
from Riegrovy Park.

**★ Church of the
Sacred Heart (F E3)**
→ Náměstí Jiřího z Poděbrad
19
Tel. 222 727 713
Visits by appointment
Vitrified brick façade, big
bell tower, huge glass clock,
large nave designed as a
single form. This is a
distinctive building (1927–
33) and the major work in
Prague by the Slovenian
architect Josip Plečník.

★ Television Tower (F E2)
→ Malherovy sady 1
Tel. 267 005 778
Daily 11am–11pm
Futuristic tower (1985–

1992) looking down
on the city from 708 ft.
Remarkable panorama
of Žižkov and Vinohrady
from its viewing platform.

★ Žižkov Hill (F E1)
In July 1420 the Hussites,
led by Jan Žižka, defeated
the forces of Emperor
Sigismund on Vítkov Hill.
In 1877, the hill was
renamed Žižkov, and in
1950 Bohumil Kafka
unveiled a monumental
equestrian statue of the
Czech patriot. Behind him,
the Constructivist National
Monument (1925–32)
stands as a symbol of the
Czech people's struggles
for independence.

BUS STATIONS

Praha–Florenc
→ Florenc subway
Departures and arrival terminal for international lines (Capital Express, Tourbus, BEI) and for internal journeys.
Information
→ Tel. 900 119 041
Tickets, bookings
The best prices are obtained from agencies such as Čedok.
Other stations
Želivského (subway line A);
Holešovice (subway line B);
Smíchov (subway line B);
Palmovka (subway line C).

RAILWAY AND BUS STATIONS

TRAIN STATIONS

Hlavní Nádraží
Prague's main station is 15 minutes on foot from Old Town Square, and on line C of the subway.
Information
→ Tel. 211 111 122
Reservations
→ From sales offices
Other stations
Nádraží Holešovice
→ Trains from northern Europe; subway line C
Smíchov
→ International trains; subway line B
Masarykovo
→ Regional lines (Bohemia, Brno and Bratislava)

With 35 comfortable rooms, bar, garden, sauna, solarium and a restaurant-gallery displaying works by Czech and Russian artists. From 2,900 Kč.

Hotel Anna (F D4)
→ Budečská 17
Tel. 222 513 111
www.hotelanna.cz
Located in a small, soberly restored Art Nouveau building with a smart pink façade, Hotel Anna offers 24 pastel-colored, simple, comfortable rooms with modern bathrooms. From 2,100 Kč – excellent value for money. The 12 rooms of the annex are slightly cheaper. The hotel's sister, the more expensive Élite, is closer to the center, on Ostrovni St (E B1, www.hotelelite.cz).

Hotel U Krále Jiřího (A C2)
→ Liliová 10
Tel. 222 220 925
www.kinggeorge.cz
Liliová is one of the most picturesque and tranquil

streets in the Old Town. Legend has it that a Knight Templar still wanders the premises with his head under his arm. The 14th-century 'King George', provides the perfect medieval setting to wait for his appearance. There are 12 rooms with beautiful dark wooden furnishings. Pub in the vaulted basement. From 3,100 Kč.

Hotel 16 (E C4)
→ Kateřinská 16
Tel. 224 919 676
A hotel on the edge of a peaceful botanic garden. Modern, attractively decorated rooms; attentive service. From 3,400 Kč.

**Pension
U Medvídků (A** C3)
→ Na Perštýne 7
Tel. 224 211 916
www.umedvidku.cz
One of the biggest and oldest beer-houses in Prague doubles as a pension with 32 basic but high-ceilinged,

very comfortable bedrooms. Characterful decor: painted ceilings, exposed beams, Gothic-style basement. One of the best bargains to be had in the city center. From 3,500 Kč.

3,500–5,000 Kč

**Pension
Dientzenhofer (D** D2)
→ Nosticova 2
Tel. 257 316 830
A small pension located in the birthplace of the greatest baroque architect Kilian Ignaz Dientzenhofer, at the end of a quiet cul-de-sac in Malá Strana. Terrace at the edge of the river Čertovka, and a view over Kampa Park: a haven of peace. From 3,700 Kč.

Dum U Velke Boty (D C2)
→ Vlašská 30
Tel. 241 098 000
At the foot of Malá Strana Park, opposite the Embassy of the United States, is this

very comfortable bedrooms. Characterful decor: painted ceilings, exposed beams, Gothic-style basement. One of the best bargains to be had in the city center. From 3,500 Kč.

attractive cottage-style hotel in a 15th-century building. All the rooms are different and are stylishly furnished. Discreet, attentive service from the owners Charlotta and Jan Rippl. From 3,760 Kč.

Hotel Evropa (E C1)
→ Vaclavské námestí 25
Tel. 224 228 117
www.evropahotel.cz
Czech Secession style at its most luxurious and decadent. The Evropa may have lost its sheen, but its charm persists in the heavy revolving door, the wooden elevator, ceramic balconies and stunning wrought-iron staircase. However, the 90 rooms are of uneven quality. Magnificent café (open to non-guests). From 4,000 Kč (with bath).

Hotel Cloister Inn (A C3)
→ Konvitská 14
Tel. 224 211 020
Only the name suggests that it is built on the foundation of a medieval monastery.

Ruzyně airport

13 miles west of Prague.
Tel. 220 113 314

Links to city center

Bus Line nº 119
Every 10 mins, to Dejvicka subway (A, green line); 45-mins trip; 12 Kč (single)

Bus Line nº 100
In front of main terminal, to Zlicin subway (B, yellow line); 12 Kč (single).
For both buses buy tickets before boarding.

Čedaz private van service
→ *Shared taxi. Counter in the Arrival Hall. Approx. 360 Kč (20-mins trip).*

Taxi Fix Car
→ *500–700 Kč (20-mins trip). Possibility of sharing.*
Several hotels offer the airport transfer.

PRAGUE RUZYNĚ · 21 km · PRAGUE

AIRPORT

Except where otherwise indicated, the prices given are for a double room with bathroom, breakfast included, in high season (Christmas–Jan 2, April–June, Sep–Nov). Rates are slightly cheaper in July-Aug. Many hotels have a limited number of rooms so advance reservation is essential. Reductions may be offered when reservations are made on the Internet. Some hotels set their prices in line with the current Euro value, so the prices quoted may vary accordingly.

1,000–2,500 Kč

Unitas Pension (A C3)
→ *Bartoloměiská 9*
Tel. 224 221 802
For anybody wishing to spend a night in the cell where Vaclav Havel once slept (room P6). The former convent, later a secret police prison under the Communist regime, is now run by nuns and has regained its serenity. There are 28 rooms (for 1, 2, 3 or 4 people). Double room: 1,400–2,000 Kč.

Pension Avalon (A D2)
→ *Havelská 15*
Tel. 224 228 083
In a 15th-century house near Saint Havel's Market. Small, simple but clean rooms, all with bathrooms. Young clientele (possibility of sharing rooms for 4/5 people). 1,400–1,700 Kč.

Pension City (F B4)
→ *Belgická 10*
Tel. 222 521 606
Náměstí Míru subway
Quiet, well-equipped rooms, but old-fashioned decor. 2,320 Kč.

Pension Větrník
→ *U Větrníku 40*
Tel. 220 513 390
Tram nº 18 (30-mins trip)
You only need half an hour to escape from the center and breathe some country air. Six large guest rooms (big beds, cozy down duvets) in an 18th-century mill owned by Miloš Opatmý. Medieval cellar (or courtyard in summer) for authentic Czech meals by a fireplace. Reservation essential. From 2,000 Kč.

2,500–3,500 Kč

Pension U lilie (A C2)
→ *Liliová 15* Tel. 222 220 432
An anonymous entrance and charming sunny courtyard a few minutes from Charles Bridge. The 17 rooms are simple but bright (with bathroom). Pleasant restaurant. 2,800–3,600 Kč.

Hotel Lunik (F B4)
→ *Londýnská 50*
Tel. 224 253 974
The 'Cold War' realism of the Lunik's façade still stands out, but the hotel, privatized and renovated, offers a friendly welcome.

TAXIS

A fare scale (displayed on the front doors) has been introduced, but Prague's taxis are still unreliable.
→ *Starting fare 30 Kč then 22 Kč/km (waiting 4 Kč/min)*

Companies
The following companies speak English.

AAA Taxi
→ *Tel. 222 333 222*

Halotaxi
→ *Tel. 222 135 111*

CARS

Driving is not advisable in the center (pedestrian areas, one-way streets).

Alcohol levels
Zero tolerance of drinking and driving.

Speed
50 km/hr in town; 90 km/hr in rural areas; 130 km/hr on freeway.

Parking
Three paying zones from Mon-Sat 8am–6pm.

Orange zone
→ *Price 10 Kč/15 mins, 40 Kč/1hr (limit 2 hrs)*

Green zone
→ *Price 30 Kč/hr, 120 Kč/6 hrs (limit 6 hrs)*

Blue zone
→ *Residents and businesses*

Parking lots
City center
→ *Price 30 Kč/hr, approx. 340 Kč/day*

Outskirts (P+R)
→ *Supervized parking Price 10 Kč/day.*

Infringements
Clamp: phone the number indicated on the ticket; the authorities remove it for a minimum of 500 Kč.

Transportation and hotels in Prague

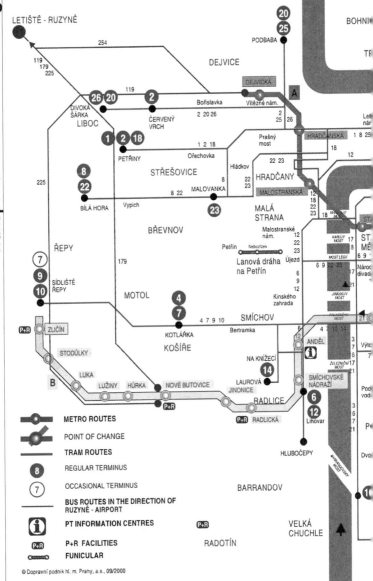

© Dopravní podnik hl. m. Prahy, a.s., 09/2000

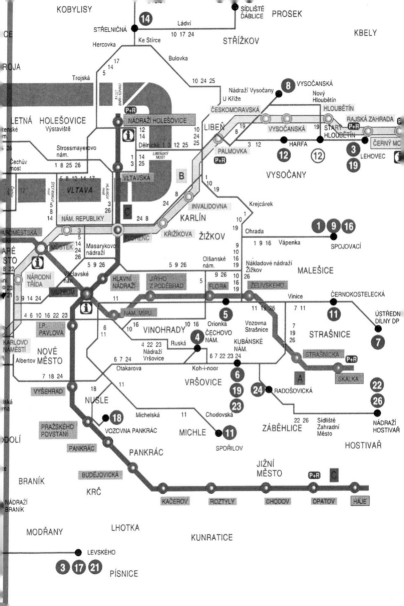

RUZYNĚ AIRPORT

rague's latest designer
otel is a nine-story
modern building in a prime
location, and set around a
gloriously landscaped
courtyard. The interior is
contemporary, too, with
lots of stone, steel and
glass. All 110 rooms have
facilities now taken for
granted in this type of
hotel: DVD, CD players,
satellite TVs, high-speed
internet connections, etc.
Rooms on the top floors
have floor-to-ceiling
windows, with views of the
Castle. From 6,500 Kč.

Crowne Plaza
→ Koulova 15
Tel. 224 393 111 Trams
n° 20, 25; Dejvická subway
An interesting example
of the Stalinist style
renovated in 1996, with
some realist friezes
exalting Soviet heroism.
Monumental proportions
inside, but with all the
Western comfort. 8,300 Kč.

Hotel Hoffmeister (**C** E3)
→ Pod Bruskou 9
Tel. 251 017 111
Situated between the river
and the Castle, this elegant
mansion is reminiscent of
a fine country home. The
former master of the place
was Adolph Hoffmeister,
painter, diplomat and
friend of Chaplin, Dali and
Picasso. Good restaurant ,
Ada. 7,500–9,400 Kč.
Hilton Atrium (**B** F3)
→ Pobřežní 1
Tel. 224 841 111
This big glass cube, built in
1990, is a symbol of the
change in regime that took
place the year before. The
country's biggest hotel
(788 rooms) is centered
around a huge atrium.
Plants, fountains and
marble punctuate the
communal areas. Special
rates available. 9,000 Kč.
Hotel Paříž (**A** F1)
→ U Obecního Domu 1
Tel. 222 195 195

www.hotel-pariz.cz
The place for Art Nouveau
enthusiasts – the lobby is
a work of art in itself. The
rooms are modern, well
equipped, if on the small
side. You must visit the
restaurant Sarah
Bernhardt: with its gold
wainscoting, it is truly
superb. From 10,500 Kč.
Four Seasons (**A** F1)
→ Veleslavínova 2a
Tel. 222 427 000
There are 12 five-star hotels
in Prague and the Four
Seasons is probably the
most attractive. Right on
the Vlatav river, on the
edge of the Old Town, it
has sweeping views of the
city. Opened in 2001 after
years of construction and
renovation, it combines
four buildings – classical,
Renaissance, baroque and
modern – and it has the
level of comfort of all FS
hotels: unbeatable.
From 10,500 Kč.

PUBLIC TRANSPORTATION

Tramway
→ Daily 4.30am–midnight
24 lines. Night trams
numbered 51 to 58 with
central stop in Lazarská
(every 30 mins).
Subway
→ Daily 5am–midnight
(every 2 mins, 4–10 mins
off-peak)
Three lines: A (green),
B (yellow) and C (red).
Buses
→ Daily 4.30am–midnight
Serve the outskirts. Night
buses numbered 501 to
514 (every 30 mins) from
Lazarská.
Cable car (Cog tramway)
→ Winter: daily 9.15am–
8.45pm; summer: daily
9am–11.30pm (every 10–
15 mins). Price 12 Kč.
Climbs Petřín hill.
Leaves from Újezd, also
stops in Nebozízek.
Fares
Tickets
→ 8 Kč (valid for 15 mins
in bus and tram or for
four subway stations)
→ 12 Kč (1 hr unlimited
travel on entire network)
Sold singly or in cards at
kiosks, tobacco stores
and hotels. Singly in
machines.
Travel pass
→ 70 Kč/1 day, 200 Kč/3
days, 250 Kč/7 days,
280 Kč/15 days
Available in PIS and DP
offices or in subway.
Prague Card
→ 690 Kč/3 days
See the Welcome to
Prague! pages.
Reductions / Free
Free for under 6-yr-olds,
50% for 6–12-yr-olds.
Information
→ Tel. 296 191 817

RUZYNĚ AIRPORT

VNÍ NÁDRAŽÍ (CENTRAL STATION)

SUBWAY (MŮSTEC STATION, LINE A)

73 rooms are modern well-equipped. 4,500 Kč.

tel Sax (D C2)
lánský Vršek 328/3
257 531 268
ellent location in the
art of Malá Strana. Light
d space are the watch-
rds here. Twenty-two
dern rooms, organized
und a superb atrium and
h views of the rooftops of
Strahov Monastery and
Castle. From 4,500 Kč.

000–6,000 Kč

**sidence Domus
nrící (C** B4)
Loretánská 11
220 511 369
mall hotel for those in
arch of a restful stay,
touched by the bustle
the center. The seven
ge and splendid rooms
e suite) are tastefully
nished and open onto a
ge south-facing terrace.
00–6,000 Kč.

U Zlatého stromu (A C2)
→ Karlova 6
Tel. 222 220 441
www.zlatystrom.cz
The 'Golden Tree' is on the King Road, in the heart of the Old Town. Vaults, recesses, mezzanines, pale wooden furnishings: 19 distinctive rooms and three suites, spread over a centuries-old house. Cozy atmosphere, subdued lighting and an unbeatable view of Charles Bridge. There is a restaurant on the ground floor (tables in the gorgeous inner garden in summer) and a disco in the 13th-century cellars. 5,000–5,500 Kč.

Hotel Adria (E C1)
→ Vaclavské nám. 26
Tel. 221 081 200
www.hoteladria.cz
The Adria offers two aspects of Prague from its snug interior: a gleaming façade on Wenceslas Square or the charm of a quiet Franciscan garden.

Remarkable restaurant, the Triton, decorated as a grotto with extravagant neo-baroque rocks. Modern, well-equipped bedrooms; Internet facilities.
From 5,300 Kč.

U krále Karla (C B4)
→ Úvoz 4
Tel. 257 532 869
www.romantichotels.cz
Four-star hotel located at the foot of the castle, the 'King Charles' was part of the Benedictine order in 1639 and still has Gothic-Renaissance decor, vaulted and coffered ceilings, stained-glass windows, chandeliers etc. Three suites with fireplace and 16 comfortable rooms. From 5,500 Kč.

Hotel Kampa (D D3)
→ Všerhdova 16
Tel. 257 320 508
A former 17th-century armory with a Gothic interior decor worthy of a Walt Disney movie set: a profusion of

colorful arms, armor and chandeliers. The 85 bright rooms are more discreet than the communal areas. Excellent Czech cooking in the restaurant and terrace b the Vltava. From 6,500 Kč.

OVER 6,500 Kč

**Romantik
Hotel U Raka (C** A3)
→ Černínská 10
Tel. 220 511 100
www.romantikhotels.com/Pra
The only preserved wooder house (end of 18th century) in Prague. Former stables were converted into six pretty rooms, with natural materials and flowers. One suite has a winter garden and a fireplace. The hotel is much sought-after, so reserve well ahead. From 6,500 Kč.

Hotel Josef (B C4)
→ Rybná 20
Tel. 221 700 111
www.hoteljosef.com

Thematic index

Letters (**A**, **B**, **C**...) relate to the matching sections. Letters on their own refer to the spread with useful addresses. Letters followed by a star (**A★**) refer to the spread with the fold-out map and places to visit. The number **1** refers to the double page **Welcome to Prague!**

SHOPPING

Bookshop
Anagram **A**
Crafts
Boema **C**
St Havel's Market **1**, **A**
Decoration / Design
Café Patio **E**
Modernista **A**
Galerie Peron **D**
Department stores/ shopping centers
Bilá Labut' **1**
Koruna Palác **1**, **E**
Kotva **1**, **B**
Pavilón **F**
Tesco **1**
Fashion
Lucerna pasáž (Galery mody) **E**
Salánek królovny Žofie **C**
Food
Holešovice Market **1**
Kotva **B**
Pavilón **F**
St Havel's Market **1**, **A**
Galleries
Galerie Benoni **C**
Galerie Peron **D**
Josef Sudek Galerie **B**
Velryba **E**
Glassware
Boema **C**
Icons
Icons gallery **C**
Markets
Fleamarket **1**
Holešovice Market **1**
St Havel's Market **1**, **A**
Musical instruments
Antique music instruments **C**
Natural products
Botanicus **B**
Puppets

Galerie Marrionetta **D**
Records
Rock Café **E**
Koruna Palác (Bonton) **E**

CZECH CUISINE

Czech pubs/wine bars
Hostinec Stará radnice **C**
Pivnice Radegast **A**
Pivnice U Sv. Tomáše **C**
Švejk **B**
U Černého vola **C**
U Dvou Koček **A**
U Fleků **E**
U Golema **B**
U pinkasů **E**
U Vystřeleného oka **F**
Restaurants
Čertovká **D**
Kammený Most **A**
Klub architektů **A**
Lví dvůr **C**
Nebozízek **D**
Peklo **C**
Ponte **E**
Renthauz **C**
U Cisaru **C**
U modré růže **A**
U modré kachničky **D**
U sedmi Švábů **D**
U zlaté hrušky **A**
Fish, seafood
Hanavský pavilón **B**
Rybí trh **B**

WORLD CUISINE

American
Bohemia Bagel **D**
French
Ambiente **F**
Bazaar Mediterranée **D**
Bistrot de Marlène **E**
Chez Marcel **B**
La Perle de Prague **E**

La Provence **B**
Indonesian
Sate **C**
International
Čertovka **D**
Dynamo **E**
Kammený most **A**
Kozička **B**
Mlýnec **A**
Nebozízek **D**
Pravda **B**
Tower Praha Restaurant **F**
U Cisaru **C**
Velryba **E**
Italian
Peklo **C**
Pizzeria Grosseto **F**
Mediterranean
Pasha **D**
Tex-mex
Cantina **D**
Red, Hot and Blues **B**

CAFÉS, TEAROOMS

Cafés
Akropolis Caf **F**
Barock **B**
Dolce Vita **B**
Kavárna Medúza **F**
Kavárna Obcení dům **A**
Odkolek **A**
Palác Akropolis **F**
Potrefená Husa **F**
St Nicholas café **D**
Cafés / Tearooms
Café Slavia **E**
Café Louvre **E**
Café Patio **E**
Dobrá Cajovna **E**
Kajetánka **C**
Konvikt **A**
Malý Buddha **C**
U Zavěšenýho kafe **C**
Internet café

Spika Internet Café **1**, **F**

GOING OUT

Festivals
Autumn Festival **1**
International Jazz Festival **1**
Mozart in Prague **1**
Prague Spring **1**
Bars
Banana Café **B**
Divadelni bar / Mala scena **F**
Double trouble **A**
Kaaba Café **F**
Kozička **B**
Marquis de Sade **B**
Palác Akropolis **F**
U malého Glena **D**
U sedmi vlků **F**
Velryba **E**
Zanzi Bar **D**
Discotheques
FX radost **F**
Karlovy lázné **A**
Roxy **B**
Jazz, blues
Agharta **E**
Lucerna music Bar **E**
Malostranská Beseda **D**
Reduta **E**
U malého Glena **D**
Rock
Lucerna music Bar **E**
Malostranské beseda **D**
Palác Akropolis **F**
Rock Café **E**
Uzi **F**
Theaters / Opera
Divadlo V. Celetné **1**
National Puppet Theater **1**
State Opera **F★**
Ta Fantastika **1**
Theater of the Estates **A**
Vinohrady Theater
see Náměstí Míru **F★**